The
Interpreter's Guidebook
Techniques for programs and presentations

FOURTH EDITION

Jim Buchholz • Brenda Lackey • Michael Gross • Ron Zimmerman

Interpreter's Handbook Series

An interpreter on the island of Efate, Vanuatu, leads visitors on a guided walk through the native forests.

UWSP FOUNDATION PRESS, INC.
UNIVERSITY OF WISCONSIN-STEVENS POINT
STEVENS POINT, WI 54481

UWSP Foundation Press, Inc.
University of Wisconsin-Stevens Point
Stevens Point, WI 54481

Library of Congress Cataloging-in-Publication Data

Buchholz, Jim, 1978- author.
  The interpreter's guidebook : techniques for programs and presentations. -- Fourth edition / by Jim Buchholz, Brenda Lackey, Michael Gross, Ron Zimmerman.
     pages cm -- (Interpreter's handbook series)
  Previous edition by Kathleen Harris Regnier.
  Includes bibliographical references and index.
  ISBN 978-0-932310-19-4
  1. National parks and reserves--Interpretive programs--Handbooks, manuals, etc. 2. Historic sites--Interpretive programs--Handbooks, manuals, etc. 3. Natural areas--Interpretive programs--Handbooks, manuals, etc. I. Lackey, Brenda, 1964- author. II. Gross, Michael (Michael P.) author. III. Zimmerman, Ronald, author. IV. Title.
  SB486.I57R44 2015
  363.6'8--dc23

                                        2014049753

Printed and bound in the United States of America by Spectra Print, Stevens Point, Wisconsin.

Ordering books: http://www.interphandbooks.org

Design: Jim Buchholz

Front cover: An interpreter leads a walk through Capilano Suspension Bridge Park in Vancouver, Canada.

Back cover: Ranger Toni Westland interacts with visitors at J.N. "Ding" Darling National Wildlife Refuge, Florida. Photo courtesy of the U.S. Fish & Wildlife Service.

This book is dedicated to the memory of lifelong interpreter

James Dorion Rooks

He followed his heart and inspired others to explore more rugged trails and wilder country. His passion and unwavering determination to protect natural places provided the catalyst that saved the Estivant Pines, Hunter's Point, and other gems of the Keweenaw Peninsula.

Photo by Doug Moore

Contents

Foreword & Acknowledgements

The Interpreter's Guidebook is the most popular book in the Interpreter's Handbook Series. It serves as a training manual for universities, agencies, nonprofit organizations, private tour companies, and other groups around the world.

The authors began discussing major revisions to *The Interpreter's Guidebook* back in 2005. The previous edition of the book was published in 1994. While the core principles and techniques were still relevant, some information (our students ask, "What are slide shows?") and photos were definitely showing their age.

Over the past ten years, we have gathered current research, ideas, and inspiration to compile this completely updated Fourth Edition. While the content has increased and the design was modernized, readers of previous editions will note that the easy-to-use style elements have been retained—concise writing, tip boxes, examples and case studies, clear organization, and numerous photos to illustrate the content.

Melding the busy lives and schedules of four individuals to collaborate, discuss, research, and ponder was no minor achievement! Some may have enjoyed being a fly on the wall during the occasional animated discussions. What is the difference between an interpretive tour and a guided walk? Who can really be considered the "first interpreter"? Are meanings truly inherent in a resource?

The depth of knowledge and broad range of experience held collectively by the authors as naturalists, field interpreters, college instructors, site managers, planning consultants, and researchers offers the reader a practical, example-laden, illustrative book that benefits anyone presenting personal interpretation programs.

This endeavor could not have been made possible without the talents and dedication of many professionals and colleagues, including the original work of our coauthor for previous editions, Kathleen Harris (Regnier). We are grateful to the many interpreters and alumni who contributed professional insights and photographs to make this book complete. They are credited at the end of each chapter.

Past and present authors who have impacted the field of interpretation provided inspiration, philosophy, and encouragement. We are thankful to our colleagues, Sam Ham, Dawn Atwell Flinn, and Brian Thill, who agreed to review the new edition of the book. Their invaluable insight and feedback led to a more practical, up-to-date, and inspirational reading for interpretive practitioners.

All readers should be especially grateful to our editors, Megan Espe, Sunshine Buchholz, and Jim Heintzman, for their talent with a red pen to make the book read cleanly and accurately.

Most importantly, we thank our significant others for their tolerance, sense of humor, and encouragement during the writing process and for their cheerful perseverance and support during our lifelong interpretive pursuits.

1

The Roots of Heritage Interpretation

> ❝ *[A poem] begins in delight and ends in wisdom.*
> Robert Frost, 1939

Heritage interpretation forges meaningful connections between people and places. Enos Mills, the father of heritage interpretation, called his fledgling profession "nature guiding," hinting at its origins. Rooted in the ancient profession of tour guiding, interpretation has been shaped over time by broad changes in society and passionate individuals eager to share their experience with others.

Enos Mills was a guide, adventurer, teacher, speaker, and wilderness activist. He is considered the father of the interpretation profession. Counting cones, circa 1921.

Origins of Guiding

Guiding ranks among the world's oldest professions. Humans have always depended on those with specific knowledge of an area to "show the way." The ascent of tourism in ancient civilizations gave rise to the profession of tour guiding, the direct ancestor of modern-day interpretation.

Prehistoric hunter-gatherer societies depended on both physical and spiritual guides to "show the way."

Hunter-Gatherer Societies: Guiding Roles

For most of human existence, people lived in hunter-gatherer societies. Small bands of 10 to 20 people depended on the bounties of nature for their survival. The role of "guiding" first developed in these prehistoric communities.

Travel in prehistoric times wasn't for recreation. Hunter-gatherers moved from place to place for survival, following food sources, finding clean water, escaping harsh weather, and avoiding competition with other groups.

Two essential roles of guiding evolved. *Pathfinder, or physical, guides* safely led their people from one place to another. They possessed intimate knowledge of the landscape, the seasons, and other tribal territories. *Mentor, or spiritual, guides* explained natural phenomena and conveyed the spiritual world, providing direction for people to achieve enlightenment and discover meanings.

After the agricultural revolution, these simple roles of pathfinder and mentor guides exploded into a multitude of specialized occupations. Pathfinders today serve as hunting guides, mountain guides, taxi cab drivers, and pilots. Mentors serve as teachers, scientists, and religious leaders. But a few professions, like interpretation, bring the pathfinder and mentor roles together.

Watch a humorous character program about the evolution of nature guiding.
www.interphandbooks.org

Nomadic hunter-gatherer societies: Roles of pathfinder and mentor guides develop

Agricultural revolution begins: More specialized occupations arise

Timeline of Interpretation History

80,000 BC

10,000 BC

Ancient Civilizations: Rise of Cultural Tour Guides

Specialized labor brought on by the agricultural revolution led to a hierarchy of social classes. Those with wealth were no longer tied to the land and could travel to other places simply for leisure or curiosity. Tourism was born.

In ancient Egypt, around 1500 BC, the first tourists left evidence of their travel in the form of graffiti. Likely the first tour guides also appeared during this time to serve travelers. In ancient Greece, starting around 500 BC, thousands of tourists risked dangerous travel by sea and land to attend national festivals such as the Olympic Games.

Mass tourism, however, developed during the ancient Roman Empire in the first century AD, spurred on by a paved road network crisscrossing the empire and an unprecedented period of peace. The increase in tourism led to a major growth in the number of professional tour guides. Popular sites like Olympia and Delphi in Greece were crowded with local guides eager to provide their services.

These early tour guides were entrepreneurs with local knowledge of the sites and mythology. They were called **periegetai** ("those who show the way around something") and **exegatai** ("those who expound or explain to"). Working for tips, the guides would lead tourists through the maze of temples, statues, and artifacts, interpreting history and legends along the way.

Popular cultural sites steeped in mythology, like Delphi in Greece, attracted crowds of ancient Roman tourists and led to the birth of professional tour guiding.

Ancient TripAdvisor.com

Not all ancient Roman tour guides were good role models for today's interpreters. Early tourists wrote about their experiences, especially if they were negative.

Over 2,000 years ago, Varro, a Roman scholar and writer, prayed:

> *Zeus, protect me from your guides at Olympia, and you, Athena, from yours at Athens.*

In the first century AD, Plutarch, a priest at the Temple of Apollo in Delphi, Greece, lamented:

> *The guides were going through their prearranged program, paying no attention to us who begged that they would cut short their monologues and their expounding of the inscriptions.*

Ancient Egypt: First tourists travel by boat up the Nile to see monuments (and leave graffiti behind)

Ancient Greece: Tourists travel by sea to festivals such as the Olympic Games; first record of tour guides

Ancient Rome: Ease of travel leads to development of mass tourism; professional tour guiding increases

| 1500 BC | 1000 BC | 500 BC | AD 1 | AD 500 |

Religious pilgrims leaving Canterbury, circa 1420.

Middle Ages: Religious Pilgrim Guides

After the collapse of the Roman Empire in AD 476, few tourists braved the crumbling and bandit-filled roads. In time, the Roman Catholic Church provided social unity and became a dominant influence. By the mid-1200s, thousands of religious pilgrims set out to experience sacred Christian sites and artifacts firsthand.

Professional tour guides again arose to assist the travelers. Religious pilgrims provided an eager audience. According to historian Maxine Feifer:

> *The guide delivered a brief historical lecture, and a pandemonium of devotion was let loose: weeping, howling, shrieking, beating of breasts, outstretching of arms, flinging of bodies on the ground.*

During the Middle Ages, guides were also hired to provide safe passage, which typically included bribes for bandits they encountered along the road. Skilled guides were highly valued, with the best being worth "half the cost of a camel."

Renaissance & Enlightenment Eras: The Grand Tour Guides

The Renaissance and Enlightenment eras spawned a resurgence in science and reason rather than faith. The study of great ancient civilizations became popular. The epitome of a young Renaissance man's education would be to experience these ancient cultural sites firsthand. The Grand Tour was a standardized travel itinerary that exposed young, upper-class men to the cultural meccas of Europe. The tour could last from several months to several years, usually dependent on how long their parents' money held out.

The young pupils were assigned a personal guide and tutor called a *cicerone*. The best guides were highly respected and sought after. They needed to be articulate, know several languages, and be well-versed in subjects such as history, literature, and architecture.

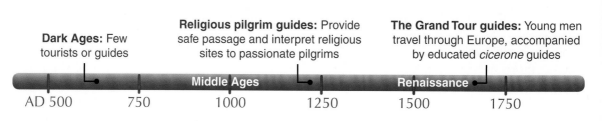

Dark Ages: Few tourists or guides

Religious pilgrim guides: Provide safe passage and interpret religious sites to passionate pilgrims

The Grand Tour guides: Young men travel through Europe, accompanied by educated *cicerone* guides

Middle Ages   Renaissance

AD 500   750   1000   1250   1500   1750

Romantic Era: Origin of Nature Tour Guides

Before the 1700s, tourism focused on cultural resources and historic sites. Nature was something to be feared and conquered. The wilderness was a place of desolation and a source of catastrophes and famine. Dark forests, misshapen mountains, and roaring waterfalls were hazards to be avoided.

As the Industrial Revolution changed landscapes into cities of factories and smog, people began to yearn for places that were untouched and pure. Romantics sought to free themselves from the unemotional rationality of the Enlightenment, and they found this freedom in the purity of nature. Wilderness was no longer something to be feared but rather an ideal to be explored, admired, and respected. The Alps mountain range in Europe became the center of a new type of tourism based on natural sites and resources.

By the 1760s, day trips were being organized out of Geneva, Switzerland, for the express purpose of viewing glaciers and waterfalls. Local hunters became the first guides to lead tourists into the mountains. They understood nature, told good stories, and imparted interesting information. In addition to mountaineering, the guides offered one-hour and nine-hour day hikes through the valley forests and along streams. They were the first true nature guides, those who focused on natural phenomena instead of just cultural heritage.

First Professional Guiding Organization

The mountain guides in Chamonix, France, created the first professional guiding organization in 1821. Guide candidates had to pass a licensing exam to demonstrate both their mountaineering skills and their knowledge of regional attractions, botany, and geology. A list of approved guides was posted at hotels around town. The Chamonix Guides' Company still exists.

Austrian mountain guides Anselm Klotz (left) and Josef Frey (right), prior to 1900.

First professional nature guides: Local hunters in the Alps of Europe

First professional guiding organization: Chamonix Guides' Company, France

Enlightenment | Romantic Era

1750   1780   1800   1825   1850

Nature Study Movement

The Nature Study Movement was an educational cause that became popular in the late 1800s and early 1900s. It encouraged learning through direct observation and experience in nature, rather than through textbooks and lecturing. It was hoped that students with this experience would come to a more complete understanding and appreciation of natural processes.

The nature study philosophy had a profound influence on the founders of heritage interpretation. Several significant individuals developed its basic tenets, many of which can be found in later descriptions of the interpretive profession.

Louis Agassiz is considered the father of nature study. He encouraged his students to learn using hands-on techniques.

Go to nature; take the facts in your hands; look, and see for yourself . . . The book of nature is always open. Strive to <u>interpret</u> what really exists.

Louis Agassiz (1807–1873)

Louis Agassiz, a nineteenth-century naturalist, is considered the father of nature study. He opened the first field school for teachers in 1873 in Massachusetts. Agassiz refused to be an oracle "imparting information" to his students. Instead, he required them to obtain information firsthand from specimens and their life histories. "Study nature, not books" was his motto. He wrote:

Liberty Hyde Bailey (1858–1954)

Liberty Hyde Bailey was an American botanist who founded the College of Agriculture at Cornell University. He strived to preserve American rural life and believed that nature study would strengthen rural children's interest in farming. In 1895, Cornell was funded by New York State to teach nature study in rural elementary schools. Bailey entrusted Anna Botsford Comstock to run the program.

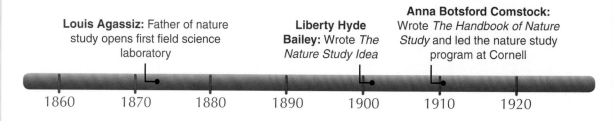

Louis Agassiz: Father of nature study opens first field science laboratory

Liberty Hyde Bailey: Wrote *The Nature Study Idea*

Anna Botsford Comstock: Wrote *The Handbook of Nature Study* and led the nature study program at Cornell

| 1860 | 1870 | 1880 | 1890 | 1900 | 1910 | 1920 |

In 1903, Bailey wrote *The Nature Study Idea*, which would be an inspiration to Enos Mills and Freeman Tilden as they defined the heritage interpretation profession. Bailey wrote:

> *Nature-study, then, is not science. It is not knowledge. It is not facts. It is spirit. It is an attitude of mind. It concerns itself with the child's outlook on the world. . . . It is not the giving of information only. We must begin with the fact, to be sure, but the lesson lies in the significance of the fact . . . . Nature-study should not be unrelated to the child's life and circumstances. It stands for directness and naturalness... Surely, the best education is that which begins with material at hand.*

Note how Bailey's quote correlates with Tilden's "Relate" principle (page 38) and Enos Mills' philosophy that nature guiding is more "inspirational than informational" (page 14–15).

Liberty Hyde Bailey brought nature study to the schools of New York State.

Anna Botsford Comstock (1854–1930)

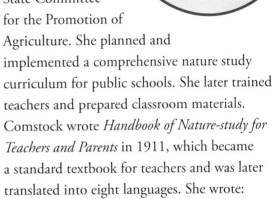

Anna Botsford Comstock grew up in New York and was an artist, educator, and leader of the Nature Study Movement. In 1895, she was appointed to the New York State Committee for the Promotion of Agriculture. She planned and implemented a comprehensive nature study curriculum for public schools. She later trained teachers and prepared classroom materials. Comstock wrote *Handbook of Nature-study for Teachers and Parents* in 1911, which became a standard textbook for teachers and was later translated into eight languages. She wrote:

> *Nature-study is, despite all discussion and perversions, a study of nature; it consists of simple, truthful observation that may, like beads on a string, finally be threaded upon the understanding and thus held together as a logical and harmonious whole.*

Note how Comstock's quote compares to Tilden's "Whole" principle (page 40).

Conservation Movement

Early American settlers viewed nature as something to be conquered and exploited. By the mid-19th century, however, much of the country's wilderness had been explored and settled. Resources, such as timber and wildlife, were being rapidly depleted. People began to realize that the wilderness and its resources were limited.

Poets, authors, and artists of the era served as interpreters of the natural world, inspiring a romanticized view of nature and encouraging Americans to preserve remnants of wilderness before they were destroyed. As a result, the first national parks, forest reserves, and wildlife refuges were established during this time.

John Muir (1838–1914)

John Muir is an icon of early preservation efforts and was an interpreter at heart. Born in Scotland, he became an inspirational naturalist, author, and advocate for preserving wilderness. He founded the Sierra Club and led the fight to save Yosemite Valley, Sequoia National Park, and other wilderness areas.

John Muir, pictured here in 1907, helped protect Yosemite Valley and shared his experiences and stories with visitors.

Muir was a fixture of Yosemite Valley and respected for his natural history knowledge, guiding skills, and vivid storytelling. Muir has been credited with being the first to use the term "interpret" when referring to nature. In an 1871 journal, he wrote:

> I'll _interpret_ the rocks, learn the language of the flood, storm and avalanche. I'll acquaint myself with the glaciers and wild gardens, and get as near the heart of the world as I can.

He also understood the teachings of the Nature Study Movement. He wrote:

> In drying plants, botanists often dry themselves. Dry words and dry facts will not fire hearts.

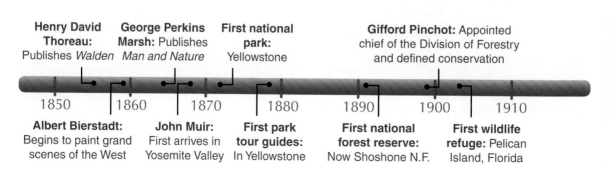

Henry David Thoreau: Publishes _Walden_

George Perkins Marsh: Publishes _Man and Nature_

First national park: Yellowstone

Gifford Pinchot: Appointed chief of the Division of Forestry and defined conservation

1850   1860   1870   1880   1890   1900   1910

Albert Bierstadt: Begins to paint grand scenes of the West

John Muir: First arrives in Yosemite Valley

First park tour guides: In Yellowstone

First national forest reserve: Now Shoshone N.F.

First wildlife refuge: Pelican Island, Florida

Early National Park Interpretation

Today's interpretation profession evolved in America's national parks. Due to the tireless efforts of preservationists, portions of the American frontier were set aside as wilderness sanctuaries. Yellowstone, with its awe-inspiring geysers, waterfalls, and canyons, became the first national park in 1872. Yosemite, protected earlier in 1854 as a state park, became a national park in 1889. From the parks' beginnings, entrepreneurs guided visitors through the rustic landscapes and interpreted extraordinary sites.

Stagecoach Storytelling

Before the 1880s, few tourists braved the rough and dangerous trip across the country to visit the early national parks. Railroad promoters saw an ideal opportunity to make the parks accessible to the masses. In 1883, the Northern Pacific Railroad began service to Yellowstone and built hotels, restaurants, and other amenities. As the number of tourists increased, so did the need for guides.

The first tour guides in Yosemite and Yellowstone were stagecoach drivers. These hardened frontiersmen with whip in hand fit the romantic vision that Americans expected from the Wild West. As they drove their "dudes" (as tourists were called) past scenic wonders, drivers spun yarns, told historical tales, and explained how natural features were formed.

Hand-colored photo of a stagecoach carrying tourists at Wylie's camp in Yellowstone, 1910.

According to a 1909 guidebook:

> *On the drive through Yellowstone Park the driver must be your guide, interpreter and friend… if you have not asked the question of some attraction that you are passing, he will call your attention to it, and pleasantly give you its story.*

In Yellowstone, the hotel porters also served as walking guides, leading visitors through dramatic thermal landscapes.

Since early guides often worked for tips—despite several attempts from park management to stop the practice of tipping—few felt the need to base their talks on scientific or historical fact. The more entertaining their presentation, the better tips they received. According to Milton Skinner in 1913, who would become the park's first naturalist a few years later:

> *[The guests] are turned over to the mercies of a porter or bell boy who has no training in guiding his clients, and what few facts he does pick up are often distorted before they reach the tourists. Then too, he is often after 'tips,' which turn his attention too much towards where he thinks the tips are coming from. The guests too are largely dependent on their stage driver. Here the trouble seems to be that the driver assumes that his passengers want to be amused and so he directs his attention to securing and giving* amusing *information rather than* accurate *information.*

While Skinner paints a rather dispiriting picture of early guides (he himself had served as a porter guide just a few years earlier), the reality is that many guides were passionate about the park resources, loved sharing their stories, and, based on journals and letters, enhanced the experience for the throngs of tourists visiting Yellowstone.

Early Yellowstone tourists on Grotto Geyser cone.

George Henderson interpreting the "Spoon" geyser, circa 1883.

George L. Henderson (1827–1905): First Park Interpreter

George Henderson has been cited as being the first true interpreter in the national parks. Henderson was hired at Yellowstone in 1882 as an assistant superintendent to protect the park from poaching and vandalism. He showed more interest, however, in being a guide than a policeman. Henderson greeted each arriving tourist party and conveyed the rules, conducted guided tours, and even gave names to the unique formations (Cupid's Cave, Painted Pool, Inspiration Point), which are still used today.

While Henderson continued the guide's traditional storytelling, he was an educated man and believed that presentations should be based on factual scientific information. In 1883, he led several groups of geologists through the formations and incorporated their expertise into his future programs and trainings. According to a visitor in 1884:

> *Mr. Henderson has lived three years at the Springs and, being a man of much scientific knowledge, rare intelligence and high appreciation of nature, he is better competent than any man living to be the guide and instructor of the [visitors].*

Visitors also praised Henderson's interpretive style that connected with a person's intellect and emotions. Another visitor in 1884 enthused:

> *Your philosophy of the Terraces satisfies the intellect. Your method of presenting them in the increasing order of interest and beauty is an art which you thoroughly comprehend.*

Henderson left his position as assistant superintendent in 1885, but he continued to serve Yellowstone as a concessionaire until 1901. He trained his own guides and drivers to lead tours with up-to-date scientific information. His philosophy of guiding still rings true:

> *When I find intelligent and appreciative visitors I give my whole soul to the subject, just as histrionic artists, musicians, or pulpit orators do. The proper presentation of the park is a fine art. Many will visit it but once in a lifetime. . . . How important, then, that there should be men capable of so presenting it as to make it the one great event of a life.*

Interestingly, Henderson was known as an "interpreter" decades before the National Park Service settled on the term. In 1905, just two months before he died, Henderson signed a letter as "the old Park interpretor."

Note how Henderson's philosophy of interpretation supports Tilden's "Art" principle (page 39).

Enos Mills, with his daughter Enda on his back, guides a group of visitors, circa 1921.

Enos Mills (1870–1922): Father of Interpretation Profession

Enos Mills is widely regarded as the father of the interpretation profession. While other entrepreneurs, like George Henderson at Yellowstone, had conducted science-based nature tours earlier, Mills was the first to recognize this new profession as "nature guiding." A nationally recognized author and lecturer, Mills described in writing his ideas and philosophies for the fledgling profession. The "nature guiding" idea became the cornerstone of the National Park Service interpretation program.

Due to health issues, Mills moved from his boyhood home in Kansas to the mountain air of Estes Park, Colorado, when he was only 14 years old. The next year, he made his first climb up 14,259-foot Longs Peak and was enamored with the mountain, beginning his long career as a guide. Over the years, he safely guided 257 groups up Longs Peak.

Mills was an avid adventurer and self-taught naturalist. He once climbed to the top of a spruce tree in a thunderstorm to feel it dance in the wind. Another time, he stumbled down from a mountain peak, stricken with snow-blindness. He met John Muir, who encouraged him to join the preservation cause and write about his adventures. He fought for the establishment of Rocky Mountain National Park, which became a reality in 1915.

In 1901, Mills purchased a ranch from a relative at the base of Longs Peak and opened it as the Longs Peak Inn. Unlike other resorts in the area, Mills' inn focused the visitor's attention on the natural world. Smoking, drinking, card playing, and dancing were prohibited.

Mills discovered that adding natural history to his guided walks inspired visitors and opened their eyes to the wonders of nature. He found inspiration largely in the nature study writings of Liberty Hyde Bailey. He called this new profession "nature guiding," to differentiate it from guides that focused on hunting and climbing. He wrote that:

> *The essence [of nature guiding] is to travel gracefully rather than to arrive . . . . A nature guide is not a guide in the ordinary sense of the word, and is not a teacher. At all times, however, he has been rightfully associated with information and some sort of education. But nature guiding, as we see it, is more inspirational than informational.*

Mills described a nature guide as:

> *A naturalist who can guide others to the secrets of nature… Touched by a nature guide the wilderness of the outdoors becomes a wonderland.*

By 1906, as his writing and public speaking engagements demanded more time, Mills began training other nature guides to lead visitors. In 1917, **Esther Burnell**, trained by Enos Mills, became the first nature guide licensed by the National Park Service to conduct interpretive tours. The next year, she became Enos' wife.

In 1920, just two years before he died, Mills wrote *The Adventures of a Nature Guide*. The book introduced the profession of nature guiding, and offered the first real definitions and philosophies that would serve as the foundation of interpretation. In it, he wrote that:

> *It is probable that nature guiding will become a nation-wide and distinct profession, and, though different, ranks with the occupations of authors and lecturers.*

Enos Mills with Esther Burnell, the first nature guide licensed by the National Park Service. They were married in 1918.

Enos Mills with Harriet Peters, the youngest visitor he guided to the top of Longs Peak.

> Note how Mills' quotes reflect the ideas of Tilden's "Reveal" and "Provoke" principles (pages 38–39).

A Nature Guiding Experiment

Stephen Mather was a businessman who made his fortune in borax. He became the director of the newly established National Park Service (NPS) in 1917. The first policy of the new bureau stated that, "The educational, as well as the recreational, use of the national parks should be encouraged in every practicable way." Education was at the core of the national park mission.

Before World War I, **Charles Goethe**, president of the California Nature Study League, and his wife, Mary, had observed nature guiding in Switzerland and other European countries. They were interested in bringing this idea of *wandervoegling*, or "nature study field excursions," back to America. In 1919, the couple personally funded a nature guiding experiment. Two well-known naturalist speakers, **Dr. Harold Bryant**, education director of the California Fish and Game Commission, and **Dr. Loye Miller**, professor of nature study at UCLA, were hired that summer to present nature programs at six resorts in Lake Tahoe, California.

Mather happened to observe one of the programs at Fallen Leaf Lake and was inspired by the size of the crowd and their enthusiasm. He convinced Bryant and Miller to organize a similar program in Yosemite National Park in the summer of 1920. Housed in tents, the men established the Yosemite Free Nature Guide Service, which included a full slate of guided walks, evening campfire talks, and office hours for answering questions. Their service became

Dr. Harold Bryant leads a nature tour in Yosemite Valley in the early 1920s.

the first comprehensive interpretive program directed by the National Park Service.

The experiment was wildly successful. After the first season, Bryant reported that "there will be sufficient demand not only to continue the work in Yosemite National Park but to extend it to other parks."

Simultaneous with the Yosemite program, ranger **Milton Skinner** was hired as the first official park naturalist in the national park system in 1920 at Yellowstone. With the aid of two

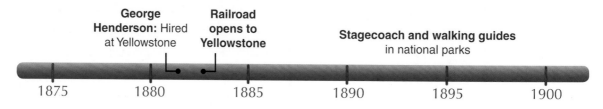

George Henderson: Hired at Yellowstone

Railroad opens to Yellowstone

Stagecoach and walking guides in national parks

1875   1880   1885   1890   1895   1900

seasonal interpretive rangers, he conducted field trips, gave lectures, and wrote natural history bulletins. Concessionaire guiding by hotel porters was abolished and replaced with "the free guide services of rangers."

In response to these successes, Mather advocated for a trained naturalist on the staff of every national park to administer educational programs. Interpretation became the duty of the federal government rather than private entrepreneurs, although park concessionaires still serve in varying interpretive capacities today.

In 1925, Bryant founded the Yosemite Field School of Natural History, a training center for nature guides. It became the foundation of the national park interpretation program. The Yosemite School and its graduates trained

thousands of park naturalists.

In 1930, Bryant was hired as the full-time assistant director of the new NPS Branch of Research and Education. He developed plans to appoint a naturalist in every national park who would create educational programs for visitors. He trained and hired interpreters for the parks. According to Bryant, the goal of interpretation was to:

> *. . . provide opportunities whereby every park visitor may learn about his environment and the laws of life. It is a program that makes education a continuous process that emphasizes vocational pursuits, that stimulates the use of leisure time for the enrichment of life.*

Yosemite Nature Guide Service, 1926. Dr. Harold Bryant (far right) established a training center for nature guides in the national parks.

Enos Mills: Begins training professional nature guides	First certified national park guide: Esther Burnell, trained by Mills	Yosemite Free Nature Guide Service established	Yosemite Field School of Natural History established	NPS Branch of Research and Education established

1905   1910   1915   1920   1925   1930

Early Cultural Interpretation in the U.S.

A licensed Gettysburg guide (left) leads an early automobile tour of the battlefield, circa 1915.

While most early tour guiding focused on cultural topics, in the United States, European immigrants didn't have much tangible history of their own to visit. The great coliseums, cathedrals, and monuments of their ancestry required a trip across the ocean. Cultural interpretation in America developed from the bloodshed of great battles and the mysterious remnants of vanished cultures.

Gettysburg Battlefield: First Licensed Guides

In July 1863, the Battle of Gettysburg ended with the largest number of casualties in the American Civil War. Nearly 50,000 soldiers were killed or wounded. Within days, grieving family members, friends, and curious visitors arrived. Local residents served as guides and escorted them to the battlefield sites.

Over time, more and more visitors arrived to witness the place of this historic turning point in the war. In January 1864, a professor at Pennsylvania College in Gettysburg wrote:

> *Since the 4th of July, many thousands of visitors have come for the purpose of taking a view of this now sacred locality, passing from point to point for the purpose of impressing upon their minds the scenes of deepest interest which were enacted here.*

As the crowds grew, so did the number of local guides. Tourists arrived by train and boarded horse-drawn wagons for day-long tours of the battlefield. Automobiles increased the traffic significantly. By 1915, about 100 private guides were giving tours of the battlefield, then under the jurisdiction of the U.S. War Department.

In response to visitor complaints, the federal government instituted a licensing program in 1915. Guides were required to take a written exam to prove their knowledge of the battle and agree to regulations covering fees, conduct, length of tours, and personal appearance.

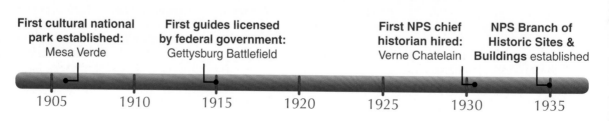

First cultural national park established: Mesa Verde

First guides licensed by federal government: Gettysburg Battlefield

First NPS chief historian hired: Verne Chatelain

NPS Branch of Historic Sites & Buildings established

1905 1910 1915 1920 1925 1930 1935

The Gettysburg Licensed Battlefield Guides was the first professional guide service in the country licensed by the federal government. The National Park Service continues to train, manage, and administer self-employed guides at Gettysburg today.

Mesa Verde: First Cultural National Park

Trappers and prospectors discovered Mesa Verde in the 1870s. Drawn by the mysterious cliff villages of a vanished culture, tourists came to climb through the ruins and collect artifacts. To curb this vandalism, President Teddy Roosevelt established Mesa Verde National Park in 1906. Its purpose was to "preserve the works of man," the first cultural national park of its kind.

Mesa Verde was a testing ground for cultural interpretation. **Jesse Walter Fewkes**, a Smithsonian archeologist, excavated and repaired many Mesa Verde ruins. He understood the importance of sharing his work with visitors. In 1908, after excavating a cliff dwelling, he wrote:

> *The impressions which a visitor obtains from it are lasting, and, if correct ones, must be of great aid in the interpretation of the structure of other ruins. . . The thought that was ever in [my] mind was to make it more attractive to visitors and to increase its educational value.*

By 1915, Fewkes was presenting popular campfire programs to visitors about his archeological work. Future archeologists and superintendents, such as **Jesse Nusbaum** (1921–46), expanded the programming at Mesa Verde to become a model of cultural interpretation.

Verne Chatelain (1895–1991): First National Park Historian

The first chief historian of the National Park Service, **Verne Chatelain**, was hired in 1931. He declared that, "Historical activity is primarily not a research program, but an educational program in the broader sense." Park historians were encouraged "to disseminate accurate information in an interesting manner." He also drafted criteria for selecting new national park historic sites based on their potential for interpreting the American story.

Chatelain summed up the national park philosophy of historic sites in 1935:

> *The task is to breathe the breath of life into American history for those to whom it has been a dull recital of meaningless facts—to re-create for the average citizen something of the color, the pageantry, and the dignity of our national past.*

The Branch of Historic Sites and Buildings was created in 1935, recognizing the essential role of historic preservation and interpretation in the National Park System.

An interpreter talks to visitors in a cliff dwelling at Mesa Verde National Park, 1939.

A Growing Profession

As resource interpretation became established in the national parks, other federal, state, and municipal agencies began adopting this model to communicate with visitors. The growing profession strove to define itself and its guiding principles.

From "Nature Guides" to "Interpreters"

Enos Mills wrote in 1920 that, "A Nature Guide is an <u>interpreter</u> of geology, botany, zoology, and natural history." However, the term *interpretation* wasn't commonly used in the early days of the profession. Prior to the 1930s, interpreters in the national parks were called park naturalists, and they conducted educational programs. During the 1930s, the term "interpretation" became more widespread as a way to distinguish park educational efforts from traditional classroom instruction. In 1940, the NPS changed the name of its education department from the Branch of Research and *Education* to the Branch of Research and *Interpretation*.

New Deal Expansion of Interpretation Programs

Park interpretive programs and personnel were greatly expanded during the Great Depression of the 1930s due to emergency federal funds and public works programs, such as the Civilian Conservation Corps (CCC) and Works

Freeman Tilden, an author and playwright, wrote *Interpreting Our Heritage* in 1957, the first book to specifically define the principles of the interpretive profession.

Progress Administration (WPA). Another surge in interpretation growth occurred after World War II ended in 1945, as returning soldiers and their families flooded into the nation's parks for recreation.

Freeman Tilden (1883–1980): Defining the Profession

Although interpretation was well established in parks throughout the U.S. by the 1940s, the profession lacked a formal definition or series of guiding principles. **Freeman Tilden** coalesced the diverse philosophies and techniques into six timeless principles that continue to guide and sustain the profession.

Tilden was an unlikely person to fill the role of defining interpretation. He wasn't a renowned naturalist, but rather a successful reporter, novelist, and playwright. However, in the early 1940s, Tilden grew tired of writing fiction and became intrigued with the country's national parks. His 1951 book, *The National Parks: What They Mean to You and Me*, was called "the best book ever written" about the parks by publisher Alfred Knopf.

During his research in the national parks, Tilden encountered many interpretive programs and media. In 1952, he wrote to NPS Director Conrad Wirth about a new idea for research:

> " *Since 1942 I have traveled many thousands of miles, visiting a great number of areas, and my conviction that the Park Service flounders in the Interpretation field has steadily grown. By this, I do not mean that it is bad; on the contrary, considering the lack of a basic philosophy, perhaps it is amazingly good; but I think the entire personnel of the National Park Service would agree with me that it is far from good enough.*

In 1954, the NPS received an Old Dominion Foundation grant in support of research designed to define the basic principles of natural and historical interpretation. Tilden was hired to conduct the study, and he traveled for years observing ranger walks, talks, media, and how visitors reacted.

In 1957, Tilden wrote *Interpreting Our Heritage*, the first book written solely to define the profession of interpretation and its underlying goals and principles. Tilden defined interpretation as:

> " *An educational activity which aims to reveal meanings and relationships through the use of original objects, by firsthand experience, and by illustrative media, rather than simply to communicate factual information.*

The six principles of interpretation that Tilden developed are as pertinent today as they were when the book was published. These principles will be explored in more depth in Chapter 2.

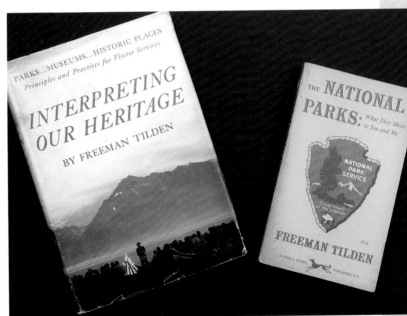

Freeman Tilden's *Interpreting Our Heritage*, 1957, and *The National Parks: What They Mean to You and Me*, 1951.

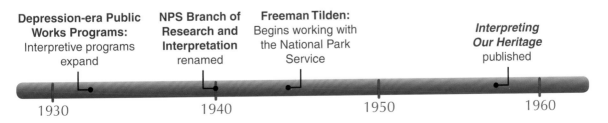

Depression-era Public Works Programs: Interpretive programs expand

NPS Branch of Research and Interpretation renamed

Freeman Tilden: Begins working with the National Park Service

Interpreting Our Heritage published

1930　　1940　　1950　　1960

The Profession Flourishes

By the end of World War II, many federal agencies, states, large municipalities, and organizations had established interpretive naturalist programs. As the number of interpretive employees grew, so did the desire for professional organizations and training.

The Birth of a National Organization

America's professional organization of interpreters, the **National Association for Interpretation (NAI)**, was created through the merger of two separate groups.

In 1954, metropolitan park district naturalists from Illinois, Indiana, Michigan, and Ohio met to create the **Association of Interpretive Naturalists (AIN)**. It became a formal organization seven years later with Charles Goethe

The Western Interpreters Association was officially formed during a meeting at Tilden Regional Park in Berkeley, California, in 1969.

and Freeman Tilden as the first honorary members. The group was composed largely of interpreters east of the Rocky Mountains and grew to 1,000 members by 1985.

In 1969, another group of enthusiastic interpreters created the **Western Interpreters Association (WIA)** to serve the western United States. Membership in this organization also grew to about 1,000 by 1985.

Although the AIN and WIA had some differences in membership and structure, most members focused on the similarities and favored consolidation. In 1988, NAI was formed as a merger of the two existing organizations. Its mission was established as:

> *Inspiring leadership and excellence to advance natural and cultural interpretation as a profession.*

The membership quickly grew to 2,300 people by 1990. In 2014, there were over 5,000 members.

NAI has developed numerous professional opportunities and benefits for its members. Annual national and regional workshops offer opportunities to learn from and network with other professionals in the field. Its magazine,

Early Association of Interpretive Naturalists (AIN) meetings took place in Bradford Woods in Indiana.

Legacy, highlights a variety of popular interpretive topics and techniques. The *Journal of Interpretation Research* serves as its outlet for scholarly peer-reviewed research.

Visit the NAI website at www.interpnet.com to discover more about the organization.

University Programs

Responding to the needs of parks and nature centers for well-educated naturalists and historians, universities and colleges emerged as training grounds for future interpretive leaders. As early as 1931, **Cornell University's** revered Nature Study curriculum included research on interpretation. By the early 1950s, the **University of Michigan** had developed a sophisticated interpretation curriculum. During the environmental activism of the late 1960s and '70s, many colleges added courses, including interpretation, that prepared students to address the demands of an empowered and environmentally sensitive public.

Numerous academic programs exist today, preparing future interpreters through courses in natural and cultural history, biology, communication, and interpretive techniques and skills. A list of academic programs that offer interpretive curricula can be found on the NAI website at www.interpnet.com.

Students at the University of Wisconsin-Stevens Point hone their interpretive skills by leading guided walks for their peers.

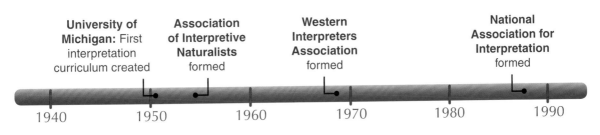

University of Michigan: First interpretation curriculum created

Association of Interpretive Naturalists formed

Western Interpreters Association formed

National Association for Interpretation formed

1940   1950   1960   1970   1980   1990

NPS Training Programs

The National Park Service has been instrumental in developing training opportunities for interpreters.

Harold Bryant founded the **Yosemite School of Field History**, which ran nearly every summer from 1925 to 1953. The seven-week course trained naturalists from throughout the country. In 1963, the **Stephen T. Mather Training Center** in Harpers Ferry, West Virginia, opened, specializing in interpretive training. Freeman Tilden himself served as an instructor here for a few years.

In 1993, the NPS launched a new training and philosophical approach called the **Interpretive Development Program (IDP)**. This introduced the importance of "connecting the interests of the visitor with the meanings of the resource." Today, the IDP continues to provide outcome-based professional development opportunities for interpreters working both within and outside the national parks. Visit http://idp.eppley.org for more information.

NAI Certification Program

Recognizing the need for training interpreters outside the national parks, NAI developed a professional certification program in 1998 that provides recognition of an interpreter's knowledge and skills. The goals are to improve competency of professional interpreters and create a standard for knowledge of interpretive principles, practices, and skills. The certification program provides valuable opportunities for interpreters at all levels to gain consistent preparation for their interpretive efforts. Visit www.interpnet.com to learn more.

Zanzibar tour guide in East Africa interpreting spice groves.

A Global Profession

Wherever there are tourists, interpreters are there to guide them. Professional associations have proliferated to serve these interpreters around the globe. The United Kingdom has been a leader in the field since 1975 with the establishment of the **Association for Heritage Interpretation**. **Interpretation Canada** began in 1978. A list of international organizations is available at www.interphandbooks.org. As Enos Mills wrote in *The Adventures of Nature Guide*, "May the tribe increase!"

Guide at Poas Volcano National Park in Costa Rica.

Documenting Interpretation

Since the writings of Enos Mills and Freeman Tilden, many academics and practitioners have published resources that expand our knowledge and understanding of heritage interpretation. Resources used for writing this book are listed at the end of each chapter. Some "must-read" books are included below. A list of online and digital resources can be found at www.interphandbooks.org.

An Interpreter's Library

A good interpreter's library includes a rich collection of books about nature, history, and communication techniques. Here is a list of must-read books for front-line interpreters:

- *The Adventures of a Nature Guide* (1920) by Enos Mills. The first description and philosophy of nature interpretation in a park setting.

- *Interpreting Our Heritage* (1957) by Freeman Tilden. The foundational book that set definitions and principles still used in the interpretive profession.

- *Interpreting the Environment* (1976) by Grant W. Sharpe. The first classroom textbook to focus on the principles and methods of interpretation.

- *Interpreting for Park Visitors* (1980) by William Lewis. A compact book that provides practical strategies for communicating with audiences.

- *Personal Interpretation: Connecting Your Audience to Heritage Resources* (2002) by Lisa Brochu and Tim Merriman. A concise book that shares examples, approaches, and techniques from more in-depth resources.

- *Interpretation of Cultural and Natural Resources* (2003) by Doug Knudson, Ted Cable, and Larry Beck. A comprehensive textbook exploring the meaning, purpose, and benefits of interpretation.

- *Meaningful Interpretation: How to Connect Hearts and Minds to Places,* *Objects, and Other Resources* (2003), edited by David Larsen. A workbook developed for the National Park Service filled with questions and exercises that assist in creating thematic and meaningful programs.

- *Conducting Meaningful Interpretation: A Field Guide for Success* (2006) by Carolyn Ward and Alan Wilkinson: A comprehensive guide of modern theories, techniques, and strategies for effective interpretation.

- *Handles: A Compendium of Interpretive Techniques to Help Visitors Grasp Resource Meanings* (2012) by Peggy Ann Scherbaum. A practical listing of effective interpretive techniques and examples that front-line interpreters can use in programming.

- *The Gifts of Interpretation*: *Fifteen Guiding Principles for Interpreting Nature and Culture* (2012) by Larry Beck and Ted Cable. Expands on Tilden's original principles and provides modern ideas for developing programs and communicating with audiences.

- *Interpretation: Making a Difference on Purpose* (2013) by Sam Ham. Provides practical and theoretical foundations for why effective interpretation works.

References

Origins of Guiding

- Cable, T. (2012). Musings on the history of professional nature guiding. *International Interpretation Newsletter, Q3.* Retrieved from http://www.internationalinterpretation.org
- Casson, L. (1974). *Travel in the ancient world.* Baltimore, MD: Johns Hopkins University Press.
- Feifer, M. (1985). *Tourism in history: From Imperial Rome to the present.* Briarcliff Manor, NY: Scarborough House.
- Perrottet, T. (2003). *Pagan holiday: On the trail of ancient Roman tourists.* New York, NY: Random House, Inc.
- Pond, K. L. (1993). *The professional guide: Dynamics of tour guiding.* New York, NY: Van Nostrand Reinhold.

Nature Study Movement

- Bailey, L. H. (1911). *The nature-study idea.* New York, NY: The Macmillan Company. Retrieved from http://books.google.com
- Comstock, A. B. (1922). *Handbook of nature study.* Ithaca, NY: Comstock Publishing Company. Retrieved from http://books.google.com

Early National Park Interpretation

- Brockman, C. F. (1978, January). Park naturalists and the evolution of National Park Service interpretation through World War II. *Journal of Forest History, 24–43.*
- Drummond, A. (2002). *Enos Mills: Citizen of nature.* Boulder, CO: University Press of Colorado.
- Mackintosh, B. (1986). *Interpretation in the National Park Service: A historical perspective.* Washington, D.C.: National Park Service. Retrieved from http://www.cr.nps.gov/history/online_books/mackintosh2/

- Mills, E. (1920). *The adventures of a nature guide.* Garden City, NY: Doubleday, Page & Company.
- National Park Service & Yosemite Natural History Association (1960). Nature guide service: 1920–1960 [Special issue]. *Yosemite Nature Notes, 39*(7). Retrieved from http://www.yosemite.ca.us/library/yosemite_nature_notes
- Whittlesey, L. H. (2007). *Storytelling in Yellowstone: Horse and buggy tour guides.* Albuquerque, NM: University of New Mexico Press.

Early Cultural Interpretation in the U.S.

- Fewkes, J. W. (1908). *Report on excavation and repair of the Spruce Tree House, Mesa Verde National Park, Colorado, in May and June, 1908.* Washington, D.C.: Government Printing Office.
- Jacobs, M. (1864, January). Later rambles over the field of Gettysburg. *United States Service Magazine, 69–72.*
- Lawhon, K. (2012, July 12). Go with a Licensed Battlefield Guide. *The Blog of Gettysburg National Military Park.* Retrieved from http://npsgnmp.wordpress.com/2012/07/12/go-with-a-licensed-battlefield-guide/
- Mackintosh, B. (1986). *Interpretation in the National Park Service: A historical perspective.* Washington, D.C.: National Park Service. Retrieved from http://www.cr.nps.gov/history/online_books/mackintosh2/
- Sellars, R. W. (2007, Spring). A very large array: Early federal historic preservation—the Antiquities Act, Mesa Verde, and the National Park Service Act. *Natural Resources Journal (47),* 267–328.

A Growing Profession

- Mackintosh, B. (1986). *Interpretation in the National Park Service: A historical perspective.* Washington, D.C.: National Park Service.

Retrieved from http://www.cr.nps.gov/history/online_books/mackintosh2/

- Tilden, F. (1957). *Interpreting our heritage.* Chapel Hill, NC: The University of North Carolina Press.

The Profession Flourishes

- Merriman, T. & Brochu, L. (2006). *The history of heritage interpretation in the United States.* Fort Collins, CO: InterpPress.
- Sharpe, G. W. (1976). *Interpreting the environment.* New York: John Wiley & Sons.
- Weaver, H.E. (1976). Origins of interpretation. In G.W. Sharpe (Ed.), *Interpreting the environment* (pp. 28-51). New York, NY: John Wiley & Sons.

Image Citations

All photos copyright of the authors unless noted below. Images published prior to 1923 and by federal agencies are in the public domain.

- Pp. 2–3: Enos Mills climbing a tree, reprinted by permission of Enos Mills Cabin Collection
- P. 4: Neanderthal family, artist's rendition of Earth approximately 60,000 years ago, courtesy NASA/JPL-Caltech
- P. 5: Veduta of Delphi, with a sacrificial procession, by Claude Lorrain, ca 1645
- P. 6: Lydgate and pilgrims leave Canterbury, *Siege of Thebes*, attributed to Gerard Horenbount, ca 1516–1523
- P. 7: Austrian mountaineers and guides, *Lechtaler Impressionen*, taken prior to 1900
- P. 8: Portrait of Jean Louis Agassiz, 1870
- P. 9: Portrait of Liberty Hyde Bailey, ca 1913
- P. 9: Portrait of Anna Botsford Comstock, ca 1904
- P. 10: Portrait of John Muir, ca 1902
- P. 11: Stagecoach at Wylie's camp, 1910, NPS photo
- P. 12: Tourists on Grotto Geyser cone, NPS photo

- P. 13: George Henderson and Mrs. Aven Nelson and daughters at the Spoon Geyser, ca 1883, American Heritage Center, University of Wyoming-Laramie
- P. 14: Enos Mills leading visitors, reprinted by permission of Enos Mills Cabin Collection
- P. 15: Enos Mills with Esther Burnell, the Denver Public Library, Western History Collection, F-20897
- P. 15: Enos Mills with Harriet Peters, reprinted by permission of Enos Mills Cabin Collection
- P. 16: Dr. Harold Bryant leading a nature tour, NPS photo
- P. 17: Yosemite Nature Guide Service, 1926, NPS photo
- P. 18: Tourists in a Ford Model T at the "Devil's Den" at Gettysburg, ca 1910–1915, courtesy of William Creswell (CC BY 2.0)
- P. 19: Tourists at cliff dwellings in Mesa Verde National Park, Library of Congress, Prints & Photographs Division, FSA/OWI Collection, [LC-USF33-012347-M3]
- P. 20: Freeman Tilden, NPS photo
- P. 22: AIN and WIA meeting photos, National Association for Interpretation archives

Website Resources
www.interphandbooks.org

Video Clip

- **Pilgrimage to the Past: Discovering Interpretation's Guiding Roots.** Humorous character interpretation that traces the evolution of the interpretive profession from ancient guides.

Online Readings

- Several historic books, documents, and articles that describe the foundations of heritage interpretation.

2
Meaning-Centered Interpretation

> *If the doors of perception were cleansed everything would appear as it is, Infinite.* William Blake, 1793

Interpreters play an important role in society. They work at sites that have been preserved because they hold exceptional meaning as our natural and cultural heritage. People come to these places in search of meanings. The professional interpreter facilitates this process, opening doors to knowledge, insight, and inspiration—the perceptions of those meanings that make a place special.

An interpreter at the Washington Island Art and Nature Center in Wisconsin interacts with a young visitor.

What is Heritage Interpretation?

Interpretive bird talk at Schmeeckle Reserve, Wisconsin.

To many, the term "interpreter" means someone who translates foreign languages or uses sign language. At its basic premise, a "heritage interpreter" is a translator of sorts, translating the technical language of natural and cultural history into a message that everyone can understand.

But heritage interpreters are more than just translators. Many widely used definitions have been proposed in an attempt to capture the essence of heritage interpretation, including:

Freeman Tilden (1957):

An educational activity which aims to reveal meanings and relationships through the use of original objects, by firsthand experience, and by illustrative media, rather than simply to communicate factual information.

National Park Service (2001):

A catalyst in creating an opportunity for the audience to form their own intellectual and emotional connections with the meanings and significance inherent in the resources.

National Association for Interpretation (2002):

A mission-based communication process that forges emotional and intellectual connections between the interests of the audience and meanings inherent in the resource.

Interpretation: Making a Difference on Purpose by Sam Ham (2013):

A mission-based approach to communication aimed at provoking in audiences the discovery of personal meaning and the forging of personal connections with things, places, people, and concepts.

Each of these definitions provides insight into common elements of an interpretive experience, including:

1. Interpretation is a **communication** process
2. Interpretation deals with tangible **resources** (objects, artifacts, things, places, landscapes)
3. Interpretation is presented to recreational **visitors** (audiences)
4. Interpretation is based on facilitating the visitor's search for **meanings** (relationships, connections, significance)

What's the Best Definition?

Freeman Tilden encouraged interpreters to reflect and create their own definitions:

" *The true interpreter will not rest at any dictionary definition . . . a definition is too inclusive, or it fails to emphasize that which we believe is vital. As to the concepts given above, I should hope that the interpreter will have others of his own, doubtless just as valid and just as stimulating.*

A Meaning-Centered Model

This book explores a meaning-centered philosophy of interpretation encapsulated in this definition:

> **Heritage interpretation is a communication process that guides visitors to discover meanings in objects, places, and landscapes.**

Interpretation is based on meanings. Meanings are at the core of every interpretive experience. To better understand and apply this philosophy, a Meaning-Centered Model describes the interaction between the key components of an interpretive experience. Visitors, resources, and the interpreter interact to produce meaningful experiences.

Canadian naturalist and author Yorke Edwards summarized the interpretation process:

> *The ingredients in the interpretation process consist of a communicator, something to be interpreted, and an audience. All three are necessary for interpretation to happen. But the catalyst that makes interpretation happen once the stage is set is the art of the interpreter. With no art there is no interpretation.*

Visitors

Resources

Meaningful Experiences

Interpreter

Schmeeckle Reserve, Wisconsin.

South Carolina Aquarium.

Visitors

Interpretation is fundamentally different than other types of education processes because the audience is composed of **visitors**—people at leisure who are recreating in parks, natural areas, nature centers, and public land management areas; zoos, aquariums, arboretums, and public gardens; farms and industrial sites; museums; cultural and historic sites. Visitors are autonomous; they are self-directed, free-choice learners in a recreational setting. They "re-create" themselves through the experiences they choose.

Resources

People visit interpretive sites and facilities to experience **resources.** Resources are the tangible natural and cultural features of an interpretive site that serve as icons for meaning. They are also the collections of specimens and artifacts housed in museums, the animals in zoos and aquariums, and the plants in botanical gardens and arboretums. A strong knowledge of resources is essential to present an effective and credible interpretive program that is meaningful to visitors.

Visitor Characteristics

- ▸ People attend a program as part of their recreational experience.
- ▸ Visitors are autonomous.
- ▸ They bring with them varied backgrounds and diverse levels of education and experience.
- ▸ Visits occur within a personal and social context; shared experiences are often critical in constructing meaning.

Resources Characteristics

- ▸ Objects (specimens, artifacts), places, and landscapes.
- ▸ Tangible characteristics that can be perceived by the senses.
- ▸ Mean different things to different people.

Milwaukee Public Museum, Wisconsin.

Governor Mike Huckabee Delta Rivers Nature Center, Arkansas.

Interpreter

An **interpreter** is a professional, seasonal employee, or volunteer who guides visitors in their search for meaning in natural and cultural resources. They may have the title of interpreter, docent, guide, naturalist, or educator, but their common link is that they facilitate informal learning. Interpreters are artists, blending factual information with a diversity of creative techniques to engage and inspire their audiences. They must be knowledgable about both the resources they interpret and the audiences that receive their messages.

Interpreter Characteristics

▶ Facilitates a visitors' search for meanings.

▶ Knowledgeable about the resource and its multiple meanings.

▶ Knowledgeable about visitors and their interests.

Meanings

❝ *[T]he dominant motivation for humans is meaning-making; the need to make meaning is innate.* ~John Falk and Lynn Dierking

Meanings are the personal connections that people make with objects, landscapes, and ideas. They are not inherent to the resource, as some definitions suggest, but rather are constructed by each person based on their cultural background, beliefs, and personal experiences. Meaningful interpretation is relevant to the experiences and interests of people. It reveals something new and is provocative and inspiring.

Meaning Characteristics

▶ Derived from but not inherent to the resource.

▶ Ascribed through social norms and cultural value.

▶ More important than information.

▶ Intangible processes, systems, ideas, values, and emotions.

Interpretation Promotes the Discovery of Meaning

Visitors come to our sites in search of meanings. Without interpretation, they can still create meaningful connections. Seeing the Statue of Liberty or the Grand Canyon for the first time is an awe-inspiring experience that doesn't require an interpretive program or media. But a well-planned interpretive experience provides a context that helps visitors discover richer and more meaningful connections to their lives.

As an example, Connie Rudd, a long-time National Park Service interpreter and supervisor, shared a story about an old pillow (a tangible resource) that someone once showed her. It is pictured below:

Without knowing anything about the pillow, think about the meanings you associate with the object. They're probably not very positive! Perhaps it taps into memories of a bad motel stay. Perhaps it represents illness or disease, or you have a sudden urge to clean.

A curator explained to Connie that there was more to this pillow than meets the eye—this was the pillow that President Abraham Lincoln

An awe-inspiring view at Canyonlands National Park, Utah, draws visitors to an overlook. People are always searching for meanings.

laid his head on when he died at the Petersen House on April 15, 1865. The stains are from his blood.

Does the pillow now mean something different to you? Has your emotional connection to the object changed? This is the power of interpretation. Just a small interpretive insight can truly change our entire perspective.

Meaning is Found in People

Communication theorist David Berlo asserts that, "Meaning is not something that we find in objects or things. Meaning is found in people." He elaborates:

▶ People can have similar meanings only to the extent that they have had or can anticipate similar experiences.

▶ Meanings are never fixed. As experience changes, meanings change.

▶ No two people can ascribe exactly the same meaning for anything. Often, the meanings aren't even similar.

▶ Communication does not consist of the transmission of meanings, but rather the transmission of messages.

▶ Meanings are not in the message; they are actively constructed by the person who hears the message.

Tangibles, Intangibles, and Universal Concepts

Good interpretation connects tangible resources with intangible meanings and universal concepts.

Tangible Resources

Interpretation is based on **tangible resources**, which are objects, places, and people that can be perceived with the senses. For example, a sugar maple tree would be a tangible object pointed out on an interpretive hike. On a larger scale, the entire forest landscape is tangible as well. Palpable facts and information are also considered tangible. For instance,

> *Sugar maples are deciduous trees found in hardwood forests of northeastern North America. Maple syrup is produced by tapping the trees for sap, and then boiling away the excess water. It takes 40 gallons of sap to make one gallon of maple syrup.*

While interpretation should always be based on well-researched information, a talk that interprets only tangibles will lack interest and inspiration for most visitors.

Intangible Meanings

For interpretation to be inspiring and relatable, it must connect to **intangible meanings** that *are not* perceived with the senses. Intangibles include processes, systems, ideas, and values that cannot be precisely comprehended. This often involves relating the resources to more ethereal stories and ideas that make us human.

Some examples:

> *During the Civil War, Northerners ate maple sugar to protest the use of black slave labor that produced cane sugar in the South.* (Intangibles: slavery, protest, war)

> *The production of maple syrup in a sugar bush brings people from different communities together in celebration of spring.* (Intangibles: community, celebration, renewal)

> *Sap is the lifeblood of a tree, carrying water, nutrients, minerals, and sugar that nourish it and keep it healthy.* (Intangibles: nourishment, health, survival, life)

When people find relevance to their own lives in a program, the "interpretive seed" has been planted successfully.

Tapping a maple tree at Conserve School, Wisconsin.

Universal Concepts

Universal concepts are the most powerful types of intangible meanings. These are the ideas, values, challenges, relationships, needs, and emotions that make up the human condition. Concepts such as community, family, health, love, home, life, and death have major significance to everyone, regardless of age, gender, ethnicity, or socioeconomic background. They provide an ideal opportunity to relate to the largest number of people in an audience.

Artists and storytellers have an intrinsic understanding of universal concepts. These are the ideas that make for a good book, song, or movie. Johnny Cash, an influential American singer-songwriter, was once asked about his favorite song topics. He answered:

> *I love songs about horses, railroads, land, Judgment Day, family, hard times, whiskey, courtship, marriage, adultery, separation, murder, war, prison, rambling, damnation,*

Johnny Cash, an American singer-songwriter, understood universal concepts and used them when writing his music.

> *home, salvation, death, pride, humor, piety, rebellion, patriotism, larceny, determination, tragedy, rowdiness, heartbreak and love. And Mother. And God.*

This quote epitomizes powerful universal concepts that help make a program meaningful.

Tangibles:

Physical resources that can be perceived with the senses or exactly comprehended.

- ▶ Objects: Collections, artifacts, specimens
- ▶ Places: Landscapes, habitats
- ▶ People: Living and past
- ▶ Palpable facts, information, narration, and chronology
- ▶ They are concrete

Intangibles:

Meanings that cannot be perceived with the senses or precisely comprehended.

- ▶ Processes: Geologic, cultural, evolutionary
- ▶ Systems: Biological, social, ecological
- ▶ Ideas: Concepts related to history, culture, and science
- ▶ Values: Significance, beliefs
- ▶ They are abstract

Universal Concepts:

Intangible meanings that have significance and relevance to everyone.

Principles of Interpretation

Freeman Tilden described six principles of interpretation in his 1957 book, *Interpreting Our Heritage.*

In 1957, Freeman Tilden established six principles of interpretation in his seminal book, *Interpreting Our Heritage.* His philosophy and principles continue to be endorsed by agencies, organizations, and academia. A thorough understanding of these principles is foundational for developing effective interpretive programs. His book is a must-read for anyone in the interpretation field.

After reading Chapter 1, the principles below should sound familiar to you. They were built from the ideas of the Nature Study Movement and from the writings of early interpretive pioneers like George Henderson, Enos Mills, and Harold Bryant.

Tilden did not mean for the principles to be viewed in isolation—rather, he wrote that they are interrelated with each building off of the others. The examples in the following section showcase how good interpretation synthesizes multiple principles at the same time.

Six Principles of Interpretation, Freeman Tilden, *Interpreting Our Heritage*, 1957

1. Relate
Any interpretation that does not somehow relate what is being displayed or described to something within the personality or experience of the visitor will be sterile.

2. Reveal
Information, as such, is not interpretation. Interpretation is revelation based upon information. But they are entirely different things. However, all interpretation includes information.

3. Art
Interpretation is an art, which combines many arts, whether the materials presented are scientific, historical, or architectural. Any art is in some degree teachable.

4. Provoke
The chief aim of interpretation is not instruction, but provocation.

5. Whole
Interpretation should aim to present a whole rather than a part, and must address itself to the whole man rather than any phase.

6. Children
Interpretation addressed to children (say, up to the age of twelve) should not be a dilution of the presentation to adults, but should follow a fundamentally different approach. To be at its best, it will require a separate program.

1. **Relate** to the experiences of visitors

> *Any interpretation that does not somehow relate what is being displayed or described to something within the personality or experience of the visitor will be sterile.*

Visitors ascribe meanings to resources based on their past experiences and cultural background. For visitors to find significance in a resource, the interpreter needs to present it in a way with which the audience members can relate. The messages must connect to their interests.

Example of Relate Principle

The interpreter drops a dime into a visitor's hand and says, "this tiny coin is heavier than the world's smallest mammal—the bumblebee bat of Thailand." The audience physically understands the minute size and weight of this creature.

2. **Reveal** meanings rather than just facts

> *Information, as such, is not interpretation. Interpretation is revelation based upon information. But they are entirely different things. However, all interpretation includes information.*

One of the basic premises of interpretation, first described by Enos Mills, is how it differs from traditional academic educational programs. Interpretation is built from factual information—the "raw material," as Tilden describes it—but it reveals the information in creative and interesting ways.

Example of Reveal Principle

Visitors are challenged to blow into the cut ends of oak blocks that have been dipped in soapy water. People blowing through red oak blocks produce foamy bubbles that froth out the end. The closed pores of white oak, however, block the passage of air and water. Since it is water tight, ship decks and whiskey barrels were traditionally made of white oak.

3. Artfully present interpretation with creative techniques

> *Interpretation is an art, which combines many arts, whether the materials presented are scientific, historical, or architectural. Any art is in some degree teachable.*

Interpreters use imagination and creative techniques to present meaningful programs, to give "form and life" to material and to "tell a story rather than recite an inventory." Thinking outside the box is essential for connecting with audiences. Like any art, interpreting comes more naturally for some, but anyone can learn to be successful with sufficient training and practice. Chapter 5 illustrates examples of creative presentation techniques.

Example of Art Principle

The audience is told they will be traveling back 10,000 years to the time of continental glaciers. Interpreters dressed as a woolly mammoth, mastodon, ground sloth, and snapping turtle compete to show that they are best adapted for survival. When the glacier melts, only one character is left standing...the snapping turtle.

4. Provoke thought and inquiry

> *The chief aim of interpretation is not instruction, but provocation.*

Visitors attending interpretive programs are primarily seeking enjoyment and inspiration, not academic instruction. The purpose of interpretation is to help the visitor "gain an understanding of the greater truths that lie behind any statement of fact." Provocation arouses thoughts, feelings, and actions. These can stimulate the visitor to greater perceptions, self-awareness, and spiritual enlightenment. At its core, a provocative program sparks curiosity in visitors and a desire to discover more.

Example of Provoke Principle

The interpreter brandishes a small propane torch and holds the flame beneath a jack pine cone. The wax on the pinecone melts, causing the fire-adapted scales to open and release seeds that helicopter to the ground at the feet of the audience. After the program, visitors understand and appreciate that fire is essential to the health of this forest ecosystem.

5. Use themes to create a **Whole**

> *Interpretation should aim to present a whole rather than a part, and must address itself to the whole man rather than any phase.*

A presentation made up of only facts is quickly forgotten. The most successful interpretive programs are created from messages that are tied together by a common thread, the big idea or theme. Tilden summarizes, "It is far better that the visitor . . . should leave with one or more whole pictures in his mind, than with a mélange of information that leaves him in doubt as to the essence of the place." Chapter 3 describes a planning process for developing thematic programs. A program should also appeal to a person's entire being—their sense of knowing, feeling, and wonder.

Example of Whole Principle

As a giant sequoia tree looms over a group of visitors, the interpreter holds up a seed about the size of a pea. She says, "The largest living organism by volume begins as this tiny seed. Consider the amazing stories this 1,800 year old tree could tell . . . of birth, growth, destruction, and death."

6. Present **Children's** programs based on developmental stages

> *Interpretation addressed to children (say, up to the age of twelve) should not be a dilution of the presentation to adults, but should follow a fundamentally different approach. To be at its best, it will require a separate program.*

While the theory was still in its infancy when Tilden wrote his principles, we now know that children, as they grow, pass through several cognitive developmental stages. Successful interpretive programs meet the learning abilities of children based on their developmental stage. Chapter 9 provides practical information for serving this special audience.

Example of Children Principle

Eager youngsters arrive at the afternoon program scheduled in their campground along the Mississippi River. Interpreters perform a fun interactive puppet show that dramatically conveys what life was like as a riverboat pilot. The children walk away with a new awareness about the rewards and dangers of working on the mighty Mississippi.

Goals of Interpretation

Crater Lake National Park, Oregon.

> *Through interpretation, understanding; through understanding, appreciation; through appreciation, protection.*

Freeman Tilden credits an anonymous National Park Service writer for the quote above. Heritage interpretation becomes even more important as natural landscapes and cultural treasures face increasing threats. Today, the public has an expanding role in land management decisions. Agencies value an informed public capable of supporting these decisions. Interpretation has three main goals:

Connect visitors to resources

At its core, interpretation can open visitors' eyes to a world they may have never seen before. Successful interpretation facilitates intellectual and emotional connections. While the time that interpreters spend with an audience is typically short, provocative and compelling programs plant a seed that can lead to greater involvement and understanding.

Accomplish agency/organization objectives and goals

By educating the public, interpretive programs help an agency or organization's management goals. They can shed light on controversial practices like prescribed burning or deer herd reduction. They can convey a positive image of the agency to the public.

Promote responsible visitor use and support for a site

An informed and caring public will be less likely to harm a site through vandalism, littering, or thoughtless destruction. Visitors can learn their role in fire prevention, dune conservation, or grizzly bear safety. In a larger sense, a concerned public becomes an advocate for the site, supporting officials and agency administrators when threats loom.

Goals of Interpretation

As they relate to the **visitor**:

- ▶ Provide recreation
- ▶ Heighten awareness and understanding of their natural and cultural environment
- ▶ Inspire and add perspective to their lives

As they relate to the **agency/organization**:

- ▶ Enhance the organization's image
- ▶ Encourage public participation in management

As they relate to the **site**:

- ▶ Foster proper use
- ▶ Develop advocates for the site

Distinguishing Interpretation From Education

EcoHelpers is a service learning program in Santa Monica Mountains National Recreation Area, California.

People often confuse the professions of interpretation and education as being one and the same. Freeman Tilden even called interpretation an "educational activity." But as you have discovered in the first two chapters, interpretation is its own distinct entity with unique principles and goals.

At the core of these differences is the audience. Professor and author Sam Ham initially made the distinction between "captive" and "non-captive" audiences. People in an educational setting typically attend classes and activities because they are *required to*. They are a "captive audience." People in a recreational setting, on the other hand, attend programs because they *want to*. They are a "non-captive audience."

An interpreter who understands how and why audiences differ will improve their effectiveness as a communicator. The box below highlights characteristics of each audience type.

Captive Audiences (Educational)

▶ Compulsory audience (part of a class or job expectation)

▶ Time commitment is fixed (class period or session)

▶ External rewards are important. Examples include grades, diplomas, certificates, licenses, employment, money, promotion

▶ Will accept a formal, academic approach

▶ Will make an effort to pay attention, even if bored (to earn reward)

▶ Typical settings: classrooms, job training courses, professional seminars

Non-captive Audiences (Recreational)

▶ Voluntary audience (part of a recreational experience)

▶ No formal time commitment (can leave at any time)

▶ Intrinsic rewards are important. Examples include meaning-making, fun, entertainment, self-enrichment, self-improvement, social interaction

▶ Expect an informal, creative approach

▶ Attention goes elsewhere if bored (social aspect is more important)

▶ Typical settings: parks, museums, zoos, aquariums, nature centers, extension programs, historic and cultural sites

What About Environmental Education?

Professionals have long debated whether "environmental interpretation" is its own profession or part of the broader umbrella of "environmental education." While the two share many of the same characteristics—and most people in the field are involved in both—interpretation is a distinct profession that requires a fundamentally different approach. Understanding the similarities and differences can enhance our ability to successfully communicate with all audiences at nature-based sites.

An educator leads a class of students on a hike in Portage Valley, Chugach National Forest, Alaska.

Similarities Between Environmental Education and Interpretation

▶ Most nature-based public sites and facilities, such as parks, forests, nature centers, wildlife areas, etc., conduct both types of programming.

▶ Similar natural resources and environmental topics are addressed.

▶ Both lead to greater awareness and understanding of the environment.

▶ Creative communication techniques are shared in both fields.

Differences Between Environmental Education and Interpretation

Environmental Education

▶ Captive audiences (school, youth organization, or adult learning groups)

▶ Long-term, repeat exposure (sequential learning over years)

▶ Goal is to produce an environmentally responsible citizenry (behavior change)

▶ Addresses academic standards and learner outcomes

▶ Structured teaching to achieve specific objectives and learner outcomes

▶ Audiences (classes) often share common ages, backgrounds, and expectations

Interpretation

▶ Non-captive audiences (visitors coming as part of their recreational experience)

▶ Short-term, often single programs (15 minutes to half a day)

▶ Goal is to inspire and enhance recreational experience

▶ Addresses the mission and goals of the agency or organization

▶ Less structured programs to engage and provoke

▶ Audiences are diverse in their ages, backgrounds, and expectations

What Qualities Make an Effective Interpreter?

Interpreters are an especially diverse group of people in terms of their interests and skills. However, there are common traits that all successful interpreters share:

- **They have a passion for natural and cultural resources.** Freeman Tilden wrote that the "priceless ingredient" of interpretation is love—love for the resource and love for the people who come to enjoy it. Enthusiasm and passion are contagious with the audience.

- **They desire to share their passion with others.** Interpreters are storytellers. Sharing their knowledge and ideas is what drives them.

- **They are compassionate toward their audience.** They truly care about the experience of the visitors and they strive to meet their unique needs and interests.

- **They are lifelong learners.** Interpreters rely on multiple scientific and historic fields of study. New research is published daily. Staying informed is at the root of credible interpretive programming.

- **They are creative.** Unlike an academic lecture, interpreters find creative ways to reveal messages that inspire the audience.

> **I Am An Interpreter:** Watch interpreters from around the world share their views about why interpretation matters.
>
> **www.interphandbooks.org**

Every year, the National Association for Interpretation (NAI) presents the Master Front-Line Interpreter Award to exceptional interpreters who demonstrate mastery of interpretive techniques, program development, and design of creative projects. Recent award recipients were asked to share the qualities they believe make for an effective interpreter. Their responses provide valuable insight.

Pamela Machuga (2013), Park Ranger, Cuyahoga Valley National Park, Ohio

An effective interpreter educates and inspires people in ways that connect them to the resource. Through warmth and personality they communicate with people in an engaging manner. They challenge themselves to reach out to new audiences and never stop learning about themselves and the resource.

Molly Postlewait (2010), Park Naturalist, Ernie Miller Nature Center, Kansas

Interpreters need to be willing to take a risk, to flirt with the outrageous....in costume, in design, and in facilitation of the subject. Try to give the audience something that they won't get anywhere else. Creativity is mysterious and magical. Blend the mystery and magic into your message. Don't be afraid to weave science with folklore.

Jay T. Schneider (2009), Assistant Park Superintendent, Hobbs State Park – Conservation Area, Arkansas

An effective interpreter causes excitement, has the visitor hanging on every word and asking for more. Taking the time to slow down, repeat it again, letting the visitor talk and making double sure you understand. Being easy to approach and down to earth, laughing with you, and causing you to have a life-changing moment.

Bill Lindemann (2009), Regional Interpretive Specialist, California State Parks

I believe that a good interpreter, like a good Scout, should be trustworthy (for that necessary bond with the audience), loyal (to the resource), helpful, friendly, courteous, kind, obedient (to the organizational mission), cheerful, thrifty (practicing an economy of means), brave (it takes plenty of nerve to stand before some audiences), clean, and reverent (to the planet, to the past, and to the creator).

Wren Smith (2011), Interpretive Programs Manager, Bernheim Arboretum, Kentucky

At the heart of good interpretation is the ability of the interpreter to reflect on the awesomeness of the ordinary; to grasp the potential potency from everyday encounters, whether those encounters are with other humans or the rest of nature. Most possess an artistic or poetic sensibility so that even a rusty milk pail can convey a story that connects the barnyard with the rush of modern life.

References

What Is Heritage Interpretation?

▶ Bacher, K. et al. (2007). *Foundations of interpretation: Curriculum content narrative.* National Park Service Interpretive Development Program. Retrieved from http://www.nps.gov/idp/interp/101/foundationscurriculum.pdf

▶ Ham, S. H. (2013). *Interpretation: Making a difference on purpose.* Golden, CO: Fulcrum Publishing.

▶ Mission, Vision, and Core Values. (n.d.). Fort Collins, CO: National Association for Interpretation. Retrieved from http://www.interpnet.com

▶ Tilden, F. (1957). *Interpreting our heritage.* Chapel Hill: The University of North Carolina Press.

A Meaning-Centered Model

▶ Berlo, D. (1960). *The process of communication.* New York, New York: Holt, Rinehart, & Winston.

▶ Cash, J. (1994). Liner notes. On *American Recordings* [CD]. Los Angeles, California: American Recordings.

▶ Edwards, Y. R. (1979). *The land speaks.* The National and Provincial Parks Association of Canada (Toronto).

▶ Falk, J. & Dierking, L. (2000). *Learning from museums; Visitor experience and the making of meanings.* Walnut Creek, CA: AltaMira Press.

▶ Larsen, D. (Ed.). (2003). *Meaningful interpretation: How to connect hearts and minds to places, objects, and other resources.* Eastern National.

▶ National Park Service (1997). *Compelling stories: Achieving excellence in interpretation.* Washington, DC. Retrieved from http://files.eric.ed.gov/fulltext/ED413602.pdf

Principles of Interpretation

▶ Tilden, F. (1957). *Interpreting our heritage.* Chapel Hill: The University of North Carolina Press.

Goals of Interpretation

▶ Tilden, F. (1957). *Interpreting our heritage.* Chapel Hill: The University of North Carolina Press.

Distinguishing Interpretation from Education

▶ Ham, S. H. (1992). *Environmental interpretation: A practical guide for people with big ideas and small budgets.* Golden, CO: North American Press.

▶ Ham, S. H. (2013). *Interpretation: Making a difference on purpose.* Golden, CO: Fulcrum Publishing.

Image Citations

All photos copyright of the authors unless noted below.

▶ Pp. 28–29: Courtesy of Brandon R. Bowey, Washington Island Art and Nature Center

▶ P. 30: Courtesy of Doug Moore

▶ P. 32: Touching skull: Courtesy of Brian Thill, South Carolina Aquarium

▶ P. 34: Pillow that Abraham Lincoln died on at the Petersen House, Washington, D.C. Photographs in the Carol M. High-smith Archive, Library of Congress, Prints and Photographs Division

▶ P. 35: Courtesy of Conserve School

▶ P. 36: Johnny Cash promotional picture for Sun Records, 1955

▶ P. 37: Freeman Tilden, NPS photo

▶ P. 40: Educator with children: Courtesy of Central Wisconsin Environmental Station

▶ P. 43: Courtesy of Cassie Bower, Chugach National Forest

▶ P. 44–45: Courtesy of Pamela Machuga, Molly Postlewait, Jay T. Schneider, Bill Lindemann, and Wren Smith

Website Resources
www.interphandbooks.org

Video Clip
▶ **I Am An Interpreter**. Interpreters from around the world share their views of what interpretation is and why it matters (produced by the National Association for Interpretation).

3

Planning Thematic Programs

> *You can't tell any kind of story without having some kind of a theme, something to say between the lines.* Robert Wise

The best interpretive programs are based on a creative and focused main idea that ties together the different messages shared with the audience. This main idea is called a theme. Developing a strong theme takes time and effort, but the reward is a powerful tool that is used to organize and craft meaningful programs.

An interpreter at Sleeping Bear Dunes National Lakeshore, Michigan, leads a thematic dunes hike.

Three Pillars of Interpretation

Freeman Tilden described the "priceless ingredient" of interpretation as love—having passion for the things you interpret and for the people who come to enjoy them. If you value the thing and value the people, you will make the effort to "understand them to the limits of your capacity." From that understanding, you help visitors forge meaningful connections to the resource.

Successful interpreters recognize three essential aspects of the interpretive experience: the mission and goals of their agency or organization, the interests and diversity of their visitors, and the stories of their site and resources. The combination of these ingredients define which interpretive messages and techniques will be the most meaningful and effective.

Effective interpretive messages are those that: (1) help achieve your organization's mission and goals, (2) meet the needs and interests of your audience, and (3) focus on significant site resources.

Effective Interpretive Messages

| Organization Mission and Goals | Needs and Interests of Audience | Significant Site Resources |

An interpreter talks to a large crowd at the stingray touch tank at Sea World, California.

Know Your Mission & Goals

Every agency, organization, and company has a mission—a statement of purpose that guides decision-making and provides direction. Interpretive programs must be planned to help achieve your organization's overarching goals. Mission-based presentations convey the organization's purpose to visitors and provide justification for the entire interpretive program.

Based on the mission, a program delivered by one agency or organization might differ considerably from another. For example, the National Park Service's mission is based in preservation, while the U.S. Forest Service's mission focuses on managing land for multiple purposes.

Know Your Audience

> *Your listener lives on an island—an island of his interests.* Richard Borden, 1935

Successful interpretation "builds bridges" to the islands of experiences and values that each audience member brings to a program. The best interpreters understand many facets of their visitors in order to develop programs their audience can relate to. These include their:

- ▶ Interests and expectations
- ▶ Motivations for attending
- ▶ Knowledge and experience
- ▶ Social context

Unlike educational programs where you can plan for specific ages, common interests, and similar background experiences, you likely won't know the makeup of your interpretive audience until the program starts! Interpretation focuses on people who choose to attend a program or interact with an interpreter as part of their recreational experience. Here are some tips for getting to know your audience:

Tip 1: Talk to coworkers and review market studies

While it is hard to predict the exact demographics of a recreational audience, most sites have visitor patterns that can help prepare you for your audience. For example, summer might bring in a significant number of international visitors, whereas the shoulder seasons might be dominated by local residents. A topic like "Frogs of the Park" might attract family groups, whereas a topic like "Deer Management" might attract local landowners.

If you are new to a site, talk to coworkers to get a feel for the daily, seasonal, and topic-focused audience patterns. If your site has conducted market studies, review these documents.

Tip 2: Talk to the visitors

The most direct way of knowing your audience members is to meet them. Your goal as an interpreter is to create an "interpretive conversation" with visitors rather than lecturing.

Since you typically won't know your audience until the actual program, arrive early to meet and talk with them. This practice provides valuable information for presenting pertinent messages and establishes a rapport with your visitors so they trust you and feel open to participate.

Diverse visitors attend a historic character program at Cabrillo National Monument, California.

Interpreters at Schmeeckle Reserve, Wisconsin, lead a Cross Cultural Nature Hike for international university students.

Some questions you might ask include:

- ▶ Where are you from?
- ▶ Who are you with?
- ▶ Have you been here before?
- ▶ What interested you in the program topic?
- ▶ What is your background or experience with the program topic?

The answers to these types of questions help you modify the content and delivery techniques of your program so it best relates to the visitors' backgrounds and interests. You can purposefully engage your audience by referencing things you learned from them throughout your program.

Tip 3: Meet the needs of diverse audiences

There is no "general" audience to which all interpretation applies. Each audience has unique characteristics and needs. The table on the next page highlights a few specific audience groups that require special planning. Understanding the needs of different audience types helps us create programs that are universally accessible. Often, you will have audience members from several of these groups.

Tip 4: Attract new visitors

Learning about the current audiences visiting your site is an important first step. However, identifying who is *not* coming can tell you a great deal about the limitations of the interpretive offerings. As the primary communicators at a park, natural area, or historic site, interpreters have a unique opportunity to reach out to underserved audiences and invite them to participate.

Urban youth with little exposure to nature, for example, are sometimes apprehensive about visiting more rustic parks and recreation areas. An interpreter can craft programs specifically aimed at this audience—exploratory activities that introduce their senses to the outdoors, team activities that build trust, metaphors and analogies that relate ecological processes to a more familiar urban environment.

Introducing diverse audiences to your site expands your ability to share significant messages and can lead to greater long-term support for your site and mission.

Serving Diverse Audiences

Audience	Characteristics	Interpretive Tips
Families/ Social Groups	Multiple reasons for attending interpretive programs. Time to interact with family members or friends. Learning is secondary to sharing time together.	Involve children to serve as a catalyst for whole family or group involvement. Plan activities that encourage social interaction.
Older Adults (65+)	Comprise 25–35% of interpretive audiences in national parks. Increased leisure time, diminished physical ability (mobility, hearing, sight), experienced, uninhibited, and sociable. Trend is a healthier, more active group with more money. They often return and like in-depth programs. Able to spend more time.	Avoid long or fast-paced walks. Depth perception and listening activities can be a problem. Rely on the experience of older visitors and encourage interaction and sharing.
International Visitors	Comprise about 20% of visitors to national parks of international importance (such as Yosemite and Grand Canyon). Often limited English skills, may lack knowledge of the resource. Generally younger and well educated. Frequently visit in family/social groups or tours.	Be sensitive to the cultural etiquette of each nationality. Avoid colloquial expressions and speak slowly and deliberately. Use visuals and props. Take time to learn their interests. Never assume the "common" isn't worth pointing out.
Minorities	In 2012, minorities made up 37% of the U.S. population: Hispanic and Latino Americans (16%), African Americans (13%), Asian Americans (5%), and Native Americans (1.1%). Within 50 years, minorities will be more than half of the U.S. population. They are alienated from parks and historic sites, which tend to over-represent majority traditions. In 2009, only 1 in 5 visitors to a national park was non-Caucasian.	Interpreters must learn about each minority group and how their values and traditions are represented at each site. Involve minorities in the interpretation of their own cultures and seek their input in developing programs.
People with Visual Disabilities	Nearly 60% of Americans wore glasses or contact lenses in 2013. About 2.2% of Americans reported being blind or having difficulty seeing even with glasses. This increases as people age (6.9% over 65).	Use auditory and tactile techniques. Describe props, scenes, etc. Involve via handling of objects. Ask what help they prefer if you are uncertain.
People with Hearing Disabilities	This group ranges from people who wear hearing aids to those who are legally deaf. About 17% of Americans have some degree of hearing loss. In 2012, 3.4% reported being deaf or having severe difficulty hearing. This increases as people age (15.6% over 65). Many older people have difficulty hearing in higher frequency ranges.	Use visual and tactile techniques. Those with significant hearing loss need to see the face of the interpreter in order to lip-read. Face the visitor and keep hands away from your mouth when speaking. Repeat important points and questions. Speak slowly.
People with Ambulatory Disabilities	People who use wheelchairs, crutches, leg braces, walkers, or canes. In 2012, 6.9% of Americans reported having serious difficulty walking. This increases as people age (24.3% over 65). Require equal access to facilities and programs, according to the Americans with Disabilities Act (ADA).	Select areas for talks and walks that are accessible. Avoid steep slopes, rough terrain, or historic buildings without ramps. Ask what help they prefer if you are uncertain.
People with Cognitive Disabilities	People with conditions that lead to serious difficulty concentrating, remembering, or making decisions. These include autism, Down syndrome, attention deficit disorder, and learning disabilities. In 2012, 4.9% of Americans had cognitive disabilities. This increases as people age (9.9% over 65).	Focus on people's "abilities" rather than "disabilities." Use a multisensory approach: visual, auditory, tactile. Provide concrete examples and practical applications.

Know Your Resources

People visit natural and historic sites to experience resources firsthand, whether they are site-based (like historic structures or natural features) or collection-based (like artifacts in a museum). Interpretive sites are founded to protect and manage unique resources identified in their missions. As an interpreter, it's your job to experience, study, and learn everything you can about these resources in order to share accurate and meaningful messages with visitors.

An interpreter interviews the late Bill Shea, who operated a gas station in Springfield, Illinois, during the heyday of Route 66.

Tip 1: Arm yourself with accurate information

A core premise of the profession is that information is *not* interpretation. However, effective interpretation is always built from a solid foundation of scientifically and historically correct information.

Your fact-gathering challenge is to use the processes of science that are relevant to the resources you are interpreting. As much as possible, review **primary sources**, those documents and media that were produced by eyewitnesses to or participants in the area of investigation. **Secondary sources** interpret and analyze primary sources—they are further removed from the event but make the information more accessible. **Tertiary sources** provide an overview or summary of a topic based on other sources. Be cautious using tertiary websites like Wikipedia that allow anyone to create and edit content. Always verify the accuracy of information. In the box below are examples of primary and secondary sources.

The scientific process is a search for truth, but there are always disagreements. You must be able to present multiple points of view and allow your audience to draw their own meanings. Your presentations should not be recitations of bland facts, but rather discussions of ideas of relevance, interest, and concern to the visitor.

Examples of primary sources

▶ Oral histories
▶ Diaries, journals, letters
▶ Government records
▶ Newspaper articles, news footage
▶ Interviews, speech recordings
▶ Photographs, paintings, original maps
▶ Material artifacts and specimens
▶ Published results of research studies

Examples of secondary sources

▶ Peer-reviewed articles
▶ Popular magazines
▶ Organizational reports
▶ Dissertations
▶ History books
▶ Websites with appropriate citations
▶ Biographies

Tip 2: Immerse yourself in the natural and cultural landscape

Factual information is an important starting point, but the true essence of interpretation is to connect with people's hearts and minds. Move beyond textbook facts and spend time getting to know the resource personally. You will draw on and share these experiences with visitors during programs.

For example, you can read about the unique adaptations of alpine tundra plants and how they cope with extreme conditions. But when you immerse yourself in an alpine tundra environment, your senses and perceptions come alive in a way that no book can convey. A frigid breeze on your cheek, the intense sun on your neck, the crunch of fragile rocky soil beneath your feet, the explosion of colors and textures from miniature flowers clinging to life in the vast and lonely landscape all create insights.

You also might read about the incredible engineering abilities of ancestral Pueblo people in the American Southwest. But when you visit Chaco Canyon and step inside a room in the ruins, the ancient past comes to life. You gaze up at 700-year-old fingerprints in the mud-plas-

An interpreter immerses herself in the alpine tundra of Denali State Park, Alaska.

Journaling is an ideal method to record information, thoughts, and feelings as you research and immerse yourself in the resources.

tered ceiling and feel the presence of the people who called this place home. You can almost hear the lively sounds of children playing and dogs barking.

Direct experiences shape your feelings and perceptions about a resource, which in turn help you convey messages to your audience that are rich in meaning and emotion. They help build your credibility and rapport with visitors.

Tip 3: Keep a journal

As you research your resources and become familiar with the landscape, use a journal to record all of those observations, thoughts, impressions, feelings, findings, notes, references, quotes—anything that seems relevant to the place you are interpreting. A journal is different from a diary that chronicles your personal life. Instead, it is a logbook or field notebook focusing on your interpretive resources. It becomes a rich storehouse of ideas that you can draw on as you create meaningful interpretive programs.

Planning Successful Programs

Defining a focused topic for your program requires diligent research. Make use of your local library or archives.

Understanding your site's mission and goals, audiences, and resources is a dynamic and continuous progression. Using these three elements as a foundation, you can start the process of planning interpretive programs for your visitors.

Steps to Plan Successful Programs

1. **Determine a broad topic.** Your subject should be a synthesis of the mission/goals, audience, and resources.

2. **Narrow the topic through research and brainstorming.** Use solid research and creative idea-generating techniques to learn more about the topic.

3. **Generate a list of tangibles and intangibles.** Consider both the concrete and abstract elements of your topic.

4. **Craft a strong theme.** Write a single sentence that organizes the program around tangibles and intangibles.

Determine a Broad Topic

A **topic** is the broad subject of your interpretive presentation. The most effective topics are a synthesis of the three elements you investigated in the last section. As you consider different topics, ask yourself if they:

- ▶ Help achieve the **mission and goals** of my agency or organization.
- ▶ Meet the needs and interests of my potential **audience**.
- ▶ Focus on significant cultural or natural **resources** of my site.

Choose a topic that you are passionate about; research and program development should be a fun exercise, not a chore. At times, you may be assigned program topics based on management goals (Leave No Trace ethics), behavioral issues (human/bear interactions), seasonal events (maple syrup, fall colors, spring wildflowers), or regularly scheduled programs (cave tour, historic house tour, bird hikes). Even if the topic isn't of particular interest to you, make the program your own by defining a specific theme and adding your own unique style and perspective.

Narrow the Topic through Research and Brainstorming

Once you have identified a broad subject area, your challenge is to **focus the topic** so it can be used for a concise and intriguing interpretive program.

For example, you might choose to give a talk on birds. "Birds" is obviously too broad of a topic to cover in a single half-hour or one-hour program. You might narrow the topic to a specific groups of birds, like "raptors." Continue narrowing by choosing a specific raptor, such as "Peregrine Falcons." While much more narrow than "birds," it's still a vast topic to cover well in a short period of time.

What is it about Peregrine Falcons that your program will focus on? One option could be, "Peregrine Falcons—the fastest predators in the world." Now your messages can be specific and striking. You can convey their high-speed dives,

---

Creative Topic Ideas

There are limitless focused topics for interpretive programs. Be creative and have fun. Here are a few ideas to get you started:

▶ Plants on the move (plant dispersal)
▶ Forest apartment buildings (layers of a forest)
▶ The scoop on poop (scat discovery)
▶ Alien invaders (invasive exotic species)
▶ Lights of the night (animals and plants that produce light)
▶ Dead tree real estate (importance of snags)
▶ Myths of the night sky (constellations, moon, planets)
▶ Insect insomnia (nocturnal insects)
▶ Sex in the garden (pollination)
▶ Nature's superheroes (animal adaptations)
▶ Masked bandits (raccoons)
▶ Dances with birds (courtship rituals)
▶ Nature's supermarket (edible plants)
▶ Name that tune (bird/frog songs)
▶ 'Til death do us part (symbiotic relationships)
▶ Nature's time machines (rocks)

---

illustrate how they use their feet to "club" other birds out of the air, and show the notched beak that is used to separate their prey's vertebrae.

Research the Topic

Unless you are already well-versed in your subject area, your first step is to **research the topic**. Gathering information and stories is essential for brainstorming and narrowing your program.

Most interpreters will use the Internet to begin the research process. The world wide web is an extraordinary and continuously growing resource for exploring nearly any topic. However, unlike published materials that are typically peer reviewed, the Internet is an *unregulated* resource—anyone can post anything. You should focus your search using solid academic and professional web resources, such as online journals and sites operated by universities, agencies, and scientific organizations. Be sure to document the sources of all your information.

Don't rely only on the web for your research. A variety of sources and perspectives is important to deliver a balanced view of a topic, particularly those that may be controversial. You have a responsibility to carefully research the message you are conveying.

Make use of your local public, university, or organization library. Talk directly to managers and professionals who deal with your chosen topic area. Visit your local historical society, museum, or library archive to gather information about the history of your area.

The more you research, the more confident you will be when presenting your program. You won't be able to include all of the information you gather, but you will be prepared and credible when visitors ask questions.

Brainstorm Ideas

Brainstorming is a method of generating creative ideas for more specific program topics and messages by free association of words and ideas. Successful brainstorming techniques should:

- ▶ Focus on quantity: The more ideas the better.
- ▶ Withhold criticism: Record all ideas without judgment.
- ▶ Welcome unusual ideas: Sometimes the most ridiculous thought leads to a unique program.

The following section describes different types of brainstorming techniques that you can use to generate ideas for interpretive programs.

Metaphor Session

A *metaphor* is a direct comparison between two seemingly unlike things that share some important characteristic. For example, "The tree is an apartment building for wildlife." The two unlike objects both have living spaces at different levels.

A *metaphor session* encourages interpreters to think of creative metaphors for a topic area. This works best with larger groups. During the brainstorming, one person functions as the group facilitator while another person records the group's ideas on a board or flip chart.

To begin the session, write a keyword on the board that relates to the topic. The group shouts out metaphors as fast as they come to mind without judgment. Each thought invites another. After generating a full list of metaphors, the group organizes these ideas into related thoughts. These thoughts may become the seeds of an interpretive program.

Creative brainstorming techniques help to generate ideas for specific program topics and messages.

Example of Metaphor Session

Keyword: **Wetland**

Participant Responses and Groupings:
- ▶ Sponge
- ▶ Inverted water tower
- ▶ Swimming pool

  Absorb and store excess water

- ▶ Filter
- ▶ Strainer
- ▶ Antacid

  Clean sediments and contaminants from water

- ▶ Nursery
- ▶ Birthing Clinic
- ▶ Supermarket
- ▶ Hotel
- ▶ Airport

  Provide food, shelter, and rest for wildlife

- ▶ City that never sleeps
- ▶ Nightclub
- ▶ Water park

  Active and diverse habitat

- ▶ Chapel
- ▶ Ancient Ruins
- ▶ Magic Show

  Precious, spiritual places that are disappearing

Synergistic Comparison

Synergy is the cooperative action of two or more parts. A *synergistic comparison* means finding similar characteristics between two dissimilar objects. You might generate a list like the following:

- ▶ How is a snake like a tire?
- ▶ How is a bird like an airplane?
- ▶ How is an otter like a snowmobile?
- ▶ How is a river like a person's circulatory system?
- ▶ How is a tree like an apartment building?
- ▶ How is goldenrod like McDonald's?
- ▶ How is an ecosystem like the Internet?

The less similar the objects—for example, if one is natural and one is man-made—the richer the comparison. Try to remove the cultural blinders with which we see everyday objects. Some responses from, "How is a snake like a tire?" are included in the box at right. Any of these ideas could serve as a spark for a creative interpretive program.

> **Example of Synergistic Comparison**
>
> **How is a snake like a tire?**
> - ▶ Both are thin and long when uncoiled
> - ▶ Both hiss when poked
> - ▶ Both have a textured pattern on their exteriors
> - ▶ Both have tread (belly scales) that provide traction
> - ▶ Both move over the terrain quietly
> - ▶ Both have coverings (skin/rubber) that stretch and wear out over time
> - ▶ Both have markings that can be used for identification
> - ▶ Both can be flattened on the road
> - ▶ Both become less responsive in cold weather
> - ▶ Both are common on all continents except Antarctica
> - ▶ Both have "biting ability"
> - ▶ Both are feared by some people

Mind Mapping/Clustering

Mind mapping, or *clustering*, is a technique used to map creative thinking around a central idea. It emphasizes the connection between the creativity and openness of the right side of the brain with the logic and order of the left side. Write or draw your main topic in the center of a sheet of paper or whiteboard. Then jot down the first word or phrase that comes to mind, circle it, and draw a line back to the topic. As quickly as they come to mind,

jot down other ideas associated with the main topic or brainstormed words, and connect the related thoughts with lines. Your mind map will continue to branch out like a web. When one avenue of thought is exhausted, go back to the main topic or sub-topics and start again. Each of these thoughts or idea clusters could serve as the seed for developing a creative and focused interpretive program.

Generate a List of Tangibles and Intangibles

As you discovered in Chapter 2, successful interpretation connects **tangible resources**, concrete things that we can perceive with our senses and factual information, with **intangible meanings**, abstract processes, systems, ideas, and values. The most powerful intangibles are called **universal concepts**, which are the emotions and values that make us human.

From your research and brainstorming, you have identified numerous potential topics and messages that could be incorporated into a program. Many of these are likely tangibles (facts, information, history), while others may be intangibles (stories, journals, legends, systems, ideas). Separate these ideas into tangible and intangible categories.

Some may be difficult to distinguish—for example, a "food web" is a complex system of

A tangible object, like this mosquito model, can be connected with powerful intangible meanings to which the audience can relate.

interactions (intangible) and a definable fact of ecology (tangible). Choose the category you feel it fits best.

Continue to brainstorm. What creative intangible meanings can be synthesized from the tangible information? Which intangibles would you consider universal concepts? The list of tangibles and intangibles provides the raw material for writing an effective theme (the next step).

Example of Tangibles and Intangibles

*Possible universal concepts

Focused topic: Blood-sucking behaviors of mosquitoes

Tangibles
- ▶ Females require blood protein to produce eggs
- ▶ Keen sense of smell using antennae; male antennae detect sounds
- ▶ Compound eyes detect hosts
- ▶ Biting mouth part (proboscis) adaptations
- ▶ Saliva injected as anticoagulant
- ▶ Life cycle of egg, larva (wriggler), pupa (tumbler), and adult
- ▶ Prefer some people over others based on body odor
- ▶ Carriers of disease-causing viruses and parasites, such as West Nile virus

Intangibles
- ▶ Thrill and adventure of the hunt*
- ▶ Despised by humans*
- ▶ Desire to be accepted*
- ▶ Romance of mating rituals*
- ▶ Growing up in a mosquito family*
- ▶ Survival against all odds*
- ▶ Empathy toward mosquitoes—they're not that different from us
- ▶ System of relationships among species
- ▶ Mosquitoes make it as comfortable as possible for humans to be bitten
- ▶ Suffering and pain of disease*

Craft a Strong Theme

People remember themes—they forget facts.
Sam Ham, 1992

Once you have narrowed your topic, your next step is developing a theme, or the central idea of your program. Every successful interpretive presentation has a theme. The theme provides the plot for your story. It is the thread that ties together the messages you share. It must be foremost in your mind as you plan your presentation.

Themes Versus Topics

In general, themes are more focused than topics. A topic is the main subject that you plan to interpret—for example, "the adaptations of Wisconsin owls." A theme states specifically and concisely the main idea you hope to convey to your audience—"Using keen eyesight, sensitive hearing, and silent flight, Wisconsin owls are deadly nighttime hunters." The box to the right lists more examples:

A well-written theme is a tool that will streamline your program's organization and encourage meaningful connections with your audience.

An interpreter presents a program about owl adaptations at the Raptor Education Group, Inc., Wisconsin.

Topic vs. Theme Examples

▸ **Topic:** The adaptations of woodpeckers
▸ **Theme example:** With strong sharp bills and long sticky tongues, woodpeckers serve as the *excavators* of the forest.

▸ **Topic:** The medicinal uses of cedar trees
▸ **Theme example:** White cedar, also known as the Tree of Life, saved the lives of early European explorers who were suffering from scurvy.

▸ **Topic:** Gardens of the Tower Grove Historic House
▸ **Theme example:** Inspired by gardens of his native England, Henry Shaw re-created the essence of the Old World at his home in St. Louis, the Tower Grove House.

Writing Good Themes

A good theme succinctly states the main idea of your program. It links tangible resources to appealing intangible meanings. It serves as a tool for you to stay focused and organized. David Larsen, a National Park Service interpretive trainer, suggested that a theme may be an interpreter's most powerful tool. He identified five characteristics of an effective theme:

Characteristics of Good Themes
David Larsen, National Park Service

▶ **Cohesively develops an idea or ideas.** The best way to reveal meaning is through the expression of an idea. A meaningful idea captures, organizes, and sustains the audience's attention.

▶ **A single sentence that expresses meaning.** The single sentence forces an interpreter to clearly define what they want to say in a concise way. This also makes the theme more understandable to visitors.

▶ **Links a tangible resource to intangible meanings/universal concepts.** Tangibles are physical objects, facts, and information. The goal of interpretation is to connect with visitors on an emotional, personal, or spiritual level. This is accomplished through links with intangibles and universal concepts: values, beliefs, ideas, abstractions.

▶ **Organizes an interpretive product.** The theme provides a roadmap for cohesively developing the central idea for the audience.

▶ **Expresses significance and meaning, but is not a "take-home" message.** Audiences make their own meanings. A theme is a tool for the interpreter, but whether audiences can recite it or not shouldn't be used to evaluate success.

Writing a strong, useful theme takes time and effort. Weak themes are easy to write, but they don't serve as effective tools or organizers. Here are some common pitfalls to avoid:

1. Themes that are too general.

> Timber wolves have interesting adaptations.

Your theme needs to be specific to your topic. Notice how nearly *anything* can be substituted for "wolves" in the theme. What specific adaptations will you focus on?

> The body language and vocalizations of timber wolves provide a glimpse into their complex social and family lives.

2. Themes that are "all about" something.

> The life history, adaptations, and behaviors of monarch butterflies are fascinating.

We call these "all about" themes—in this case, all about monarchs. What *doesn't* fit under this theme? You have a limited amount of time to present a focused program. Use the theme to define that focus.

> A monarch butterfly's fall migration is an epic journey filled with hazards and challenges.

3. Themes that are "sound bites."

> The underground mysteries of Lost River Cave.

While these themes sound intriguing, they are better suited as program titles for marketing. They don't serve as a good tool for the interpreter. What is the plot that will tie together these mysteries?

> The underground stream in Lost River Cave protects mysterious aquatic creatures uniquely adapted to life in the dark.

4. Themes that express purpose.

> To involve the audience in historic methods of harvesting corn.

This is a good purpose statement or objective but it doesn't define the storyline of the program. Why is it important for the audience?

> Harvesting corn by hand reveals the challenges that people faced in domesticating this grain over the past 5,000 years.

5. Themes that are not complete sentences.

> The family life and social gatherings of ancient Pueblo people.

Sentence fragments read like topics. A single, complete sentence requires you to concisely define the main message you want to convey. Verbs are powerful connectors.

> The ancient Pueblo people of Mesa Verde lived differently than we do today, yet their need for home, family, and comfort are timeless.

6. Themes that include only factual information and do not relate to the audience.

> The life cycle of an oak tree consists of an acorn sprouting, growing into a mature tree, and becoming a snag after death.

While this theme is succinct and provides direction, it doesn't have much appeal to a general audience. Find ways to relate through intangible meanings and provocation. Use personal language, active verbs, analogies, and metaphors.

> Like the life stages of a person, an oak tree is born from the earth, stretches toward the sky, reproduces and protects its offspring, and returns back to the earth.

You will typically write and rewrite your theme several times before it conveys the true essence of your message. The more time you spend writing your theme, the more focused and understandable your interpretation will be to the audience.

Professor and author Sam Ham recommends several methods for writing strong themes. Start by answering this question: "When it comes to my topic, I think it is really important for this audience to understand that _____." The answer becomes the foundation for a theme.

Then, revise the theme using the suggestions below to make it stronger:

Edit Your Theme Until It's Strong!
Sam Ham, 2013

▶ **Make them personal.** Build in personal words like "you," "we," or "us." Link to things your audience cares about. "Six different kinds of snakes live here, and knowing which is which could save your life."

▶ **Connect with things of symbolic importance.** Universal concepts such as love, family, challenge, etc. are powerful ways of connecting with the audience. "The Oregon Trail is a story of hope, struggle, and survival."

▶ **Incorporate analogies, metaphors, or similes.** Comparisons help the audience relate to resources and concepts. "Like a bulldozer, glaciers scoured the landscape, pushing rocks and gravel into massive piles."

▶ **Use verbs in an active voice, and try to avoid forms of the verb "to be."** A statement like "This landscape was sculpted by glaciers" is less active and direct than "Glaciers sculpted this landscape."

Examples of Revising Theme Statements

The statements below are actual themes written by students in an oral interpretation course. Would you consider these effective themes? If not, how could they be made stronger?

Original theme: "Dusky dolphins are very interesting mammals."

Comments: A very general theme that doesn't provide any direction. What exactly about dusky dolphins will be interpreted?

Revised theme ideas:
- ▶ "Dusky dolphins are marine mammals that have many unique adaptations that allow them to survive in a cold and salty ocean environment."
- ▶ "Dusky dolphins are marine mammals with a close-knit family group structure that is very similar to our own families."
- ▶ "The lives of dusky dolphins are plagued by vicious predators like sharks and the dangerous fishing nets of humans."

Original theme: "To inform the audience about penguins and how they may be in trouble."

Comments: Expresses the purpose of the talk rather than defining the storyline.

Revised theme idea: "Penguins are birds adapted to live in extremely frigid habitats, but global climate change is threatening their existence through habitat reduction, scarce food sources, and harsh weather conditions."

Original theme: "Dispelling the fear of mice by giving them humanistic qualities and informing of why they behave the way they do."

Comments: Narrows the topic into a compelling program idea but isn't written as a complete sentence.

Revised theme idea: "Mice are plagued with myths of being sneaky, eating cheese, and carrying disease, but their behaviors are essential in maintaining the ecosystem."

Original theme: "Snags provide habitat, food, and dens for many animals."

Comments: While this effectively focuses the scope of the program to three characteristics of snags, it doesn't include any intangible meanings. How will the audience relate to this talk?

Revised theme idea: "Snags are the apartment buildings of Schmeeckle Reserve, a place where diverse wildlife species congregate to socialize, feast, and fall in love."

Original theme: "Despite being hunted to near extinction, African elephants are intelligent, human-like animals with a folklore rooted in confusion and misunderstanding."

Comments: Narrows the topic to a few specific aspects, relates to human interests (folklore, human-like), and contains many pertinent intangibles.

A Continuous Process

Once you have written a foundational theme, you have the tool for building an organized, relevant, and meaningful program supported by creative interpretive techniques.

However, your written theme statement is never set in stone! The process of crafting themes is dynamic and mutable. As you develop your program and continue to research your topic, you will likely discover other ideas that are more central to your message and more provocative for your audience. Don't be afraid to modify your theme after it's written. Just be sure that your messages and techniques continue to support the current theme.

Theme Planning Worksheet

To streamline and organize your theme development process, we recommend using a Theme Planning Worksheet, like the blank example to the right. It includes the steps presented in this chapter followed by space to jot down your ideas. Write in pencil or save it as a computer file that can be easily changed—you want to be able to modify it as you work through the planning process.

Two completed worksheets—one focused on natural history and the other on cultural history—are also included as samples of specific program plans.

Download a blank version of this worksheet for your own theme planning.
www.interphandbooks.org

A costumed interpreter describes the life of lighthouse keepers and their families at Point Iroquois Lighthouse, Hiawatha National Forest, Michigan.

Interpretive Program Theme Planning Worksheet

Presenter Name: _____

Presentation Location: _____ **Day and Time:** _____

Program Topic: _____

Narrow your topic through research/brainstorming and write a theme:

1. List specific resources used for research: *(primary & secondary sources)*

2. List the tangible resources and intangible meanings/universal concepts of your focused topic:

    <u>Tangibles</u>   <u>Intangibles/Universal Concepts</u>

3. Program Theme: *(complete sentence, specific & focused, links tangibles to intangibles, organizational tool)*

    _____

    _____

Describe how your program will address the Three Pillars of Interpretation:

1. How will this program meet the goals of your agency or organization?

2. What audience(s) do you expect will attend? *(ages, background, interests and expectations)*

    How will you serve diverse audiences? *(people with disabilities, minorities, older adults, families)*

3. What specific site-based resource(s) will you interpret?

Interpretive Program Theme Planning Worksheet

Presenter Name: Phillip Keeper

Presentation Location: Hiawatha National Forest, MI   **Day and Time:** June 6, 10–11 a.m.

Program Topic: The lightkeepers of the Point Iroquois Lighthouse

---

Narrow your topic through research/brainstorming and write a theme:

1. List specific resources used for research: *(primary & secondary sources)*

   Brimley-Bay Mills Historical Soc, Great Lakes Lighthouse Assoc, U.S. Coast Guard
   "Growing Up at Point Iroquois in the 1920s," Betty Byrnes Bacon, 1989
   Interview with Phyliss L. Tag of Great Lakes Lighthouse Research
   Hiawatha National Forest archives of lightkeeper's logs

2. List the tangible resources and intangible meanings/universal concepts of your focused topic:

Tangibles	Intangibles/Universal Concepts
Lighthouse structure	Living as a family in a lighthouse
Lightkeeper artifacts	Joy of birth & weddings, sadness of death
Timeline history of lighthouse & keepers	Tragedy on the Great Lakes
Lightkeeper logs	Loneliness & isolation
Historic photographs of family	Light as a guiding beacon

3. Program Theme: *(complete sentence, specific & focused, links tangibles to intangibles, tool for organization)*

   The Point Iroquois Lighthouse was a home for three keepers and their families, whose togetherness forged happiness and joy from this lonely stretch of Lake Superior.

Describe how your program will address the Three Pillars of Interpretation:

1. How will this program meet the goals of your agency or organization?

   A major objective of the U.S. Forest Service is to demonstrate sustainable multiple-use management. This program showcases how the agency supports significant historic sites in addition to natural landscapes.

2. What audience(s) do you expect will attend? *(ages, background, interests and expectations)*

   Based on past program audiences: (1) family groups, interested in social interaction and hands-on activities, (2) older adults interested in history. Expect an informative, entertaining, and inspiring program.

   How will you serve diverse audiences? *(people with disabilities, minorities, older adults, families)*

   Use multisensory techniques (sight, hearing, touch). Plan walk so it is accessible to those with ambulatory limitations (climb up tower optional). Involve children. Encourage social interaction.

3. What specific site-based resource(s) will you interpret?

   Buildings (lighthouse, oilhouse, outhouse), garden site, the rooms inside the lighthouse (and what they were used for), historic artifacts found on the site that represent family (toys, oven, kerosene cans).

Interpretive Program Theme Planning Worksheet

Presenter Name: Andrea Hopper

Presentation Location: Schmeeckle Reserve, WI   **Day and Time:** May 3, 8:30–9:15 p.m.

Program Topic: Frogs in Schmeeckle Reserve

Narrow your topic through research/brainstorming and write a theme:

1. List specific resources used for research: *(primary & secondary sources)*
   First-hand experience in the wetlands
   Natural History of Amphibians and Reptiles in Wisconsin, Richard Vogt, 1981
   Seasonal records and census data from SWAMP student organization
   Wisconsin Frog and Toad Survey website, Wisconsin DNR

2. List the tangible resources and intangible meanings/universal concepts of your focused topic:

Tangibles	Intangibles/Universal Concepts
Identifying characteristics of frogs	Courtship behaviors
Unique frog songs	Competition for mates
Wetland habitat	Renewal of life in spring
Adaptations of frogs	Indicators of a healthy ecosystem
Water temperatures when species emerge	

3. Program Theme: *(complete sentence, specific & focused, links tangibles to intangibles, tool for organization)*

   As water temperatures rise, wood frogs, chorus frogs, and spring peepers emerge from their winter hibernation in Schmeeckle Reserve wetlands to engage in a spirited courtship.

Describe how your program will address the Three Pillars of Interpretation:

1. How will this program meet the goals of your agency or organization?
   The second priority of Schmeeckle Reserve is to serve as an outdoor laboratory for learning about natural communities of central Wisconsin. Frogs are an important indicator of the health of wetlands.

2. What audience(s) do you expect will attend? *(ages, background, interests and expectations)*
   Based on past program audiences: (1) university students, interested in learning the science of frogs, (2) families curious about the different calls. They expect to hear real frogs and identify them.

   How will you serve diverse audiences? *(people with disabilities, minorities, older adults, families)*
   Provide opportunities to communicate on different levels: verbal, sounds (frog calls), physical (courtship behaviors), tactile (touching frogs). Encourage discovery and exploration activities.

3. What specific site-based resource(s) will you interpret?
   Actual frogs calling (wood frogs, chorus frogs, spring peepers), wetland habitats of Schmeeckle Reserve.

References

Three Pillars of Interpretation

▶ Tilden, F. (1957). *Interpreting our heritage.* Chapel Hill: The University of North Carolina Press.

Know Your Audience

▶ Borden, R. C. (1935). *Public speaking—As listeners like it!* New York, NY: Harper & Row.

Serving Diverse Audiences *(table)*

▶ Bertnstein, R. (2012, December 12). U.S. Census Bureau projections show a slower growing, older, more diverse nation a half century from now. *United States Census Bureau.* Retrieved from http://www.census.gov/newsroom/releases/archives/population/cb12-243.html

▶ Cothran, C. C., Combrink, T. E., & Bradford M. (2005). *Grand Canyon National Park northern Arizona tourism study.* Arizona Hospitality Research and Resources Center, Northern Arizona University.

▶ Erickson, W., Lee, C., & von Schrader, S. (2014). *2012 disability status report: United States.* Ithaca, NY: Cornell University Employment and Disability Institute (EDI).

▶ Taylor, P. A., Grandjean, B. D., & Anatchkova, B. (2011). *National Park Service comprehensive survey of the American public, 2008–2009: National Technical Report.* Fort Collins, CO: National Park Service.

▶ Taylor, P. A., Grandjean, B. D., & Gramann, J. (2011). *National Park Service comprehensive survey of the American public, 2008–2009: Racial and ethnic diversity of National Park System visitors and non-visitors.* Laramie, WY: University of Wyoming, Wyoming Survey & Analysis Center.

▶ *The Vision Council fact sheet.* (n.d.). Retrieved from http://www.thevisioncouncil.org/sites/default/files/TVCFactSheet2.pdf

Craft a Strong Theme

▶ Ham, S. H. (1992). *Environmental interpretation: A practical guide for people with big ideas and small budgets.* Golden, CO: North American Press.

▶ Ham, S. H. (2013). *Interpretation: Making a difference on purpose.* Golden, CO: Fulcrum Publishing.

▶ Larsen, D. (2003) *Meaningful interpretation: How to connect hearts and minds to places, objects, and other resources.* Eastern National.

General References

▶ Falk, J. & Dierking, L. (2000). *Learning from museums; Visitor experience and the making of meanings.* Walnut Creek, CA: AltaMira Press.

▶ Lewis, W. J. (1980). *Interpreting for park visitors.* Philadelphia, PA: Eastern Acorn Press.

▶ Moscardo, G. (1999). *Making visitors mindful: Principles for creating sustainable visitor experiences through effective communication.* Champaign, IL: Sagamore Publishing.

Image Citations

All photos copyright of the authors unless noted below.

▶ Pp. 48–49: Courtesy of Dennis Yockers, Sleeping Bear Dunes National Lakeshore

▶ P. 59: Eastern Garter Snake in Spangler Park, Wooster, Ohio; photo taken by Mark A. Wilson (Department of Geology, The College of Wooster)

▶ P. 59: Tire; photo taken on the Stanlow Canalside Trail, Cheshire, England; courtesy of User Rept0n1x at Wikimedia Commons (CC BY-SA 3.0)

Website Resources
www.interphandbooks.org

Documents
▶ **Interpretive Program Theme Planning Worksheet:** Microsoft Word and Adobe PDF downloads.

4

Keys to Interpretive Communication

> *The two words 'information' and 'communication' are often used interchangeably, but they signify quite different things. Information is giving out; communication is getting through.* Sydney J. Harris

At its core, interpretation is a communication process. We often take communication for granted—it's an everyday activity like breathing air. But communicating effectively in an interpretive setting requires us to consciously apply good verbal and nonverbal methods.

An interpreter at Cumberland Island National Seashore, Georgia, communicates with body language, voice, and message.

Communicating with Visitors

Communication is the process of exchanging meaning and understanding through a common system of symbols—such as speaking, writing, or behaviors—with minimal distortion of the original message. While this sounds simple, the underlying process of communication is complex. As the facilitator of a visitor's search for meaning, an interpreter should make effective communication at the core of their duties.

Interpretation is a special form of communication. You have a unique opportunity to communicate with an audience that has free will. An array of recreational activities compete for their time—hiking, canoeing, swimming, birdwatching, eating, relaxing. When a visitor chooses to invest their valuable leisure time in your program, your job is to ensure their investment is worth it.

An interpreter communicates with a diversity of audience members at Capilano Suspension Bridge Park, Vancouver, Canada.

Interpretation strives for two-way communication between the interpreter and the audience members. The ideal program creates an "interpretive conversation" where visitors feel comfortable to ask questions and contribute their own ideas and thoughts.

Effective interpretive communication strives to create a dialogue between the interpreter and audience members.

An Interpreter's Listening Skills

When interpretive trainer Bill Lewis was asked what skills he believed would help a future interpreter, he said, "I think listening skills are extremely important." When asked why, he responded:

> *You need to listen for what people are interested in, what they want to know or what they think is important. Then you respond to **their** interests, rather than what **you** think is important.*

Communication Process

When preparing for a program, speakers often focus most of their energy on crafting the message they hope to convey. However, the message is just one of many components that interact to determine the success of communication. Due to the message being filtered through interference and the visitor's frame of reference, the message is never received exactly as sent. The goal is to have your *intended* message be as close as possible to that which is *actually* communicated.

Interpreter: Delivers *verbal* and *non-verbal messages* that can impact how the final message is received

External Interference: Factors that impede communication external to the speaker or listener—temperature, weather, external noise, or distractions

Feedback: An audience's verbal and nonverbal response to the message (frown, clap, laugh, watch the clock, ask questions)

Message: What the interpreter communicates to the visitor

Channel: The means by which a message is communicated

Internal Interference: Factors that impede communication internal to audience members— basic needs (hunger, restroom), emotional state, internal distractions (headache, other priorities)

Visitor: Receiver of the message, which is filtered through their *frame of reference*— the sum of a person's knowledge, attitudes, experience, and values

Nonverbal Communication

An interpreter delivers two types of messages: verbal and nonverbal. Our choice of words and the way that we use them affect the quality of an interpretive experience.

While we often focus on the importance of *what* we're saying, research shows that about two-thirds of communication is actually conveyed through nonverbal messages. Our facial expressions, gestures, posture, eye contact, and voice all convey meaning beyond the content of our speech.

Good nonverbal communication techniques reinforce our messages, convey emotions, and connect with people on a personal level. Poor techniques can be distracting or even contradict our message.

Confident and open body language, as demonstrated by this interpreter at Badlands National Park, South Dakota, is essential for conveying a meaningful message.

Nonverbal Communication Roles

According to professor Edward Wertheim, nonverbal communication cues play several roles that can affect the spoken message.

▶ **Repetition:** Nonverbal cues can duplicate the spoken message

▶ **Contradiction:** Cues can be in conflict with the verbal message

▶ **Substitution:** Cues can completely replace the spoken message

▶ **Complementing:** Cues can add to and strengthen the verbal message

▶ **Accenting:** Cues can emphasize or underline a verbal message

Body Language

Body language speaks louder than words. Our audience reads our gestures, posture, movement, facial expressions, and eye contact. Using body language to emphasize rather than detract from our message takes practice.

Posture/Stance

How we stand in front of the audience is a sure indication of our comfort level. Maintain a comfortable and balanced posture. Leaning slightly forward indicates engagement with the audience. Some distractive postures that should be avoided include:

▶ Leaning on objects or slumping: Conveys laziness or boredom

▶ Hands on hips: Condescending, parental

▶ Crossed arms: Disagreeing, defensive

- Hands crossed in front: Weak, timid, vulnerable
- Hands joined behind back: Condescending
- Hands in pockets: Nervous, don't know what to do with hands
- Shifting weight from foot to foot, swaying, rocking: Mental and physical discomfort
- Turning your back to the audience: Creates a physical and psychological barrier

Gestures

What should you do with your hands when giving a program? Use them! Hand gestures are excellent ways to emphasize points and demonstrate your message. Use deliberate and strong movements that are confident. When not gesturing, your hands should be at your sides, not in your pockets or crossed. Avoid repetitive gestures such as:

- Hand fidgeting
- Cracking knuckles
- Playing with rings/watches
- Twirling hair, scratching face
- Foot and finger tapping
- Holding props or notes in front of your body

These gestures can indicate to the audience that you are anxious and not well prepared.

Facial Expressions

Anthropologist Ray Birdwhistell estimated that humans exhibit and recognize around 250,000 facial expressions. They are imperative for effective communication both in the realm of personal life and public speaking. Audience members watch a speaker's face during a presentation for cues about how a speaker feels. When we're nervous, our face shows it.

Practice in front of a mirror and link your facial expressions to the messages you're communicating. Use your expressions to convey different moods such as happiness, sadness, concern, fear, surprise, and enthusiasm. Try giving your entire talk by just using facial expressions instead of speaking.

The most important tip: start your program with a smile. A smile is a universal expression that warms up the audience, shows your enthusiasm for the topic, and helps you feel more comfortable.

The body language of this interpreter at Castillo de San Marcos National Monument, Florida, showcases his approachability—his posture is balanced and engaged, his gestures are natural and open, his face is smiling and enthusiastic, and he has strong eye contact with his audience.

Eye Contact

Eye contact is an essential way to convey sincerity and credibility during a program. It connects with your audience members on a personal level. Scan the audience and let your eyes rest momentarily, about 3 to 5 seconds, on each audience member.

Maintaining eye contact is often one of the most challenging parts of public speaking. Looking into someone's eyes can make us feel exposed and vulnerable. For practice, rehearse your program with family or friends, focusing on their eyes. Also, try giving your program in a mirror while looking into your own eyes—it's not as easy as you think!

Eye contact is also important because it gives us instant feedback from the audience. If the majority of your audience looks confused or bored, you can change your presentation style to better meet their expectations.

Here are a few behaviors that can distract from effective eye contact during a program:

- ▶ Using notes or note cards—they draw your eyes away from the audience and present a barrier between you and the audience
- ▶ Talking to and looking at props—keep eye contact with the audience while the prop is displayed
- ▶ Staring at the ceiling, sky, walls, or landscape
- ▶ Focusing on just one side of the audience—the other side will feel slighted
- ▶ Focusing on one audience member or a few individuals—this makes people feel awkward

 Watch "Secrets of Body Language," a documentary by the History Channel.

www.interphandbooks.org

It is important to always have eye contact with your audience, especially when using props. Note how this interpreter at Schmeeckle Reserve, Wisconsin, is also maintaining a comfortable social space of about 10 feet with the small group.

Movement and Space

It is never ideal to stand in one place during your program. Natural movement adds a visual cue that you are engaged and enthusiastic about the topic. Walk naturally and deliberately within your presentation space. Interact with the audience. Use gestures to convey your message. Avoid repetitive movement, such as pacing, which is distracting to the audience. Punctuate the movement with stillness.

The space where you're presenting and moving is also vital. We naturally feel more comfortable speaking when we can stand behind an object. But the most effective speakers keep the space between themselves and the audi-

ence open. Don't hide behind barriers such as a podium, desk, table, or props.

In addition, we all have personal spaces where we feel comfortable interacting with others in various situations. When we step into a crowded elevator with strangers, most of us feel uncomfortable, like our personal space has been compromised. When presenting to an audience, avoid moving into the personal space of audience members. In small-group settings, a social space of 4 to 12 feet is appropriate. In large-group settings, a space greater than 12 feet feels more comfortable. The exact dimensions of comfort zones vary by culture.

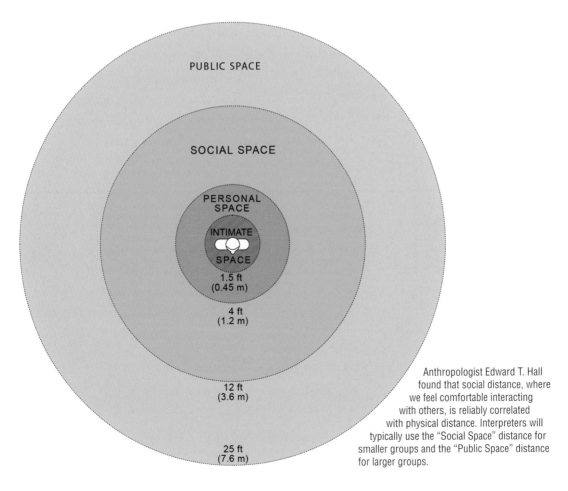

PUBLIC SPACE

SOCIAL SPACE

PERSONAL SPACE

INTIMATE SPACE

1.5 ft (0.45 m)

4 ft (1.2 m)

12 ft (3.6 m)

25 ft (7.6 m)

Anthropologist Edward T. Hall found that social distance, where we feel comfortable interacting with others, is reliably correlated with physical distance. Interpreters will typically use the "Social Space" distance for smaller groups and the "Public Space" distance for larger groups.

Voice

> ❝ *It is plain that delivery has just as much to do with oratory as with poetry. It is, essentially, a matter of the right management of the voice to express the various emotions—of speaking loudly, softly, or between the two; of high, low, or intermediate pitch; of the various rhythms that suit various subjects. These are the three things—volume of sound, modulation of pitch, and rhythm—that a speaker bears in mind.*   Aristotle, *Rhetoric*

You might spend weeks creating a profound and insightful program. But if it's presented in a monotone voice, it will fail to connect with your audience. Apart from the words, your tone of voice conveys significant meaning.

Who are the most interesting and dynamic speakers that you've heard? What makes them so inspirational? Likely, they vary their voice based on the spoken message. Exciting topics are supported by a faster, louder, and enthusiastic voice. Serious topics are presented with a slower and more deliberate tone.

For most interpretive programs, talk with the same conversational inflections that you would use with a group of friends. You're not delivering a scientific paper. Speak spontaneously and with simple directness. Your goal is to create a two-way "interpretive conversation" rather than a one-sided lecture.

Your voice is an instrument. Like any fine musical instrument, you control the **volume** (how loud you speak), the **tempo** (how quickly you speak), and the **pitch or inflection** (how high or low you speak). Beethoven's "Moonlight Sonata" arrests us with variations in pitch, volume, and rate. The unceasing monotony of elevator music, on the other hand, serves only as dull background.

Your voice must be tuned and practiced to create an effective sound. Orchestrate your talk with a contrast of high and low notes. Use the full range of your voice. Emphasize some parts of your talk with a slow, deliberate pace. Breeze lightly through other parts.

Meanings from Voice

Consider the statement, "Muskrats are the excavators of a wetland." What different meanings are conveyed when you say the phrase with emphasis on the word in bold below?

- ▶ **Muskrats** are the excavators of a wetland.
- ▶ Muskrats **are** the excavators of a wetland.
- ▶ Muskrats are **the** excavators of a wetland.
- ▶ Muskrats are the **excavators** of a wetland.
- ▶ Muskrats are the excavators of a **wetland**.

Now, try saying each of the sentences above with a different style of voice:

- ▶ Loud and triumphant
- ▶ Quiet and sincere
- ▶ Sneaky and sinister
- ▶ Humorous and sarcastic

The meaning of a simple sentence can change dramatically just based on the voice that we use.

Appearance

First impressions are critical. Without realizing it, audience members judge us at first sight based on our physical appearance: *What clothes is he wearing? What is her hairstyle? Does he look clean? Is she wearing sunglasses (and sneaking looks at me)? Is he well-groomed or unkempt?* Studies have found that appearance conveys nonverbal cues about a person's personality, cultural background, mood, level of confidence, values, and financial status.

Since most interpreters work in public settings, your appearance not only reflects you but also your organization or agency. Dress professionally and appropriately, slightly more formal than your audience. Many sites require interpreters to wear a uniform, which might be as simple as a polo shirt or as complex as a full ranger uniform.

The physical appearance of an interpreter makes an important first impression on visitors. The interpreter above is a National Park Service employee at Pearl Harbor, Hawaii. His clothes make him seem more approachable than a formally uniformed ranger.

Tips to Make a Good First Impression

▶ If you wear a uniform, be sure that it is neat and clean.

▶ If you don't wear a uniform, dress professionally and appropriately—at least a step up from your audience.

▶ Avoid wearing clothes with blatant marketing logos or phrases, such as a business trademark or a sports team logo (unless, of course, you are working for one).

▶ Don't overdress or be too formal (unless your site requires it)—you want to relate to your audience on their level.

▶ Don't wear sunglasses—eye contact is extremely important.

▶ Wear a name tag. This identifies you as the official presenter.

Watch communication expert Mark Bowden reveal the importance of body language when making first impressions.

www.interphandbooks.org

The Message

While nonverbal cues communicate emotions and confidence, the words you use form the foundation for learning and understanding. Clear, concise, relatable, provocative, thematic messages are easy for audience members to integrate into their own frame of reference. Audience members communicate their own nonverbal feedback when they understand—nodding heads, leaning forward, smiling, saying "oh" or "ah-hah." Messages that are uninspired, unorganized, and poorly spoken lead to other cues—wrinkled brows, tapping fingers, clock watching, leaning backward, yawning. Plan the message carefully, and practice nonverbal communication to deliver it with a punch!

Character interpreter Rob Nurre vividly describes the life of Increase Lapham and the influence he had on the early years of Wisconsin's conservation efforts.

Choose Your Words

Well-chosen words create vivid images. Your audience will appreciate the time you spend choosing words.

The statement, "People often shoot porcupines because they damage trees," conveys a vague image. Compare that to, "I know a woodsman from Polonia who blasts a dozen porcupines a year for stripping bark off his white pines."

Why does the second statement convey a sharper image? It refers to a specific character in a specific place with porcupines in specific trees. He doesn't just shoot porcupines, he "blasts" them, a much more active verb. The personal pronoun "I" tells us this is a real story you can vouch for. The most effective messages are spe-

cific, personal, familiar, and use active verbs and concrete nouns.

Be Specific

In interpretive programs, being specific means interpreting actual resources that visitors can experience at your site. Use specific stories and examples as much as possible. A general story about the gold rush isn't as meaningful as a specific story about Mrs. Van Winkle who in 1846 traveled by oxen across the country with her gold-seeking father to Colusa, California.

Use Active Verbs and Concrete Nouns

Active language involves the audience. Our tendency is to use many descriptors before a noun or verb. For example, "The **fast** and **agile** peregrine falcon **quickly** flew through the **beautiful** sky" is loaded with adjectives and adverbs.

Changing this to "The peregrine falcon **darted** through the **heavens**" replaces the descriptors with an active verb (darted) and a concrete noun (heavens). It conveys the same meaning but does so in a more concise and direct way.

Use Personal and Familiar Language

An important principle of interpretation is to relate to your audience's experience. Avoid technical jargon. The statement, "A woodpecker's head moves at a speed of 6 meters per second, with a force of deceleration between 1,000 and 1,600 g" is accurate, but likely not very meaningful to the general public.

Instead, use personal pronouns, personal language, and familiar terms. "When pecking, a woodpecker's head sustains forces that are over 100 times more than those felt by fighter jet pilots. How do you think their brains are protected?"

Filler Words and Pauses

When we're nervous in front of an audience, pausing to find the right word or start our next main point seems to take much longer than it really does. The silence and the stares from the audience make us uncomfortable. To compensate, we often use filler words such as *ah*, *um*, *so*, *okay*, *like*, or *you know* to fill the gaps in our speech.

Filler words disrupt the flow of a talk and make us appear unsure and unprepared. Instead of using filler words, replace them with silence. It's an uncomfortable feeling at first, but the appropriate use of pauses will make you a more credible and effective speaker.

The box at right includes several tips for using pauses effectively.

Pileated Woodpecker.

Tips for Using Pauses

❝ *The right word may be effective, but no word was ever as effective as a rightly timed pause.* Mark Twain

▸ **Use pauses for emphasis.** Moments of silence should be used to set off the main points of your talk. Pauses are like speed bumps on a road; they alert your audience that something important is coming up.

▸ **Pause when looking for a word.** When trying to think of a word or the next phrase, don't look away and say "uh" or "um." Be silent for a moment and maintain eye contact with the audience.

▸ **Take a breath.** Take a breath at the end of every major phrase or sentence. This provides more energy for your voice, helps reduce nerves, and encourages pauses.

In addition to filler words, other types of weak and unnecessary phrases can reduce your credibility and professionalism:

- **Weak words:** "Sort of," "kind of," "hopefully"
- **Disclaimers:** "It would appear..." "According to..." "Today I'll talk about..."
- **Clichés:** Overused expressions such as "a diamond in the rough" or "24/7"
- **Redundancies:** Words that mean the same thing, such as "free gift," "cooperate together," "very unique," or "personally think"
- **Gender-biased:** Avoid "you guys" to refer to your audience or "mankind" to refer to people—these have masculine connotations that can be offensive

Eliminating filler words and unnecessary phrases from your speech is a challenging process, as we naturally use these in our everyday conversations. Record yourself giving a presentation and note all of the filler words and phrases that sneak in. The next time you practice a program, make a special effort to catch the filler words and replace them with something more professional and meaningful. Over time, it will become natural to speak without the crutch of filler words.

Overusing Clichés

Author Gary Provost creatively describes the overuse of clichés in communication:

> Clichés are a dime a dozen. If you've seen one, you've seen them all. They've been used once too often. They've outlived their usefulness. Their familiarity breeds contempt. They make the writer look as dumb as a doornail, and they cause the reader to sleep like a log. So be sly as a fox. Avoid clichés like the plague. If you start to use one, drop it like a hot potato. Instead, be smart as a whip. Write something that is fresh as a daisy, cute as a button, and sharp as a tack. Better safe than sorry.

To increase credibility and professionalism, interpreters must choose their words carefully when presenting to an audience. Capilano Suspension Bridge Park, Vancouver, Canada.

Multiple Intelligences

Offering a diversity of interpretive techniques can meet the needs of different learning styles.

We all differ in how we are best able to experience and learn from the world around us. The theory of multiple intelligences, originally proposed by psychologist Howard Gardner in 1983, suggests that there are eight primary intelligences that govern how different people best acquire information.

By understanding the various forms of intelligences, you can develop interpretive techniques that meet the diverse learning needs of visitors coming to your programs. It is important to engage as many of these learning preferences as possible.

 Watch Dr. Howard Gardner describe his theory of multiple intelligences.

www.interphandbooks.org

Serving Multiple Intelligences in Interpretive Programs

Intelligence Type	Learning Preferences	Interpretive Techniques
Visual-Spatial	Prefer learning through visuals or observations	Pictures, map activities, art projects, 3-D models, images, videos, charts, puzzles, and spatial understanding
Linguistic-Verbal	Prefer learning through words, both in speech and writing	Creative writing, poetry, journals, storytelling, word games, debating
Logical-Mathematical	Prefer learning through logic, reasoning, and systems	Graphs, data, number games, problem solving, scientific experiments
Bodily-Kinesthetic	Prefer learning through the use of body, hands, and touching	Hiking, using tools, interpretive dance, building models, charades, acting, movement games
Musical (aural)	Prefer learning through sound, patterns, and rhythms	Instruments, singing, recordings, listening activities, rhythm activities
Interpersonal (social)	Prefer learning in groups or with other people	Group projects, skits, mentoring
Intrapersonal (solitary)	Prefer to work alone and use self-reflection and analysis	Reflective writing, independent study, assessing personal strengths
Naturalistic	Prefer to learn by finding patterns and relating information to natural surroundings	Classifying natural forms (such as animals, plants, rocks), nature observations, exploring nature

Establishing Credibility

Credibility is the feeling of trust and respect that you inspire in your audience. As an interpreter, you establish your credibility by showing the audience that you know what you are talking about. This is often done by sharing your experiences that relate to the topic or explaining why you are passionate about the topic. Either way, your program must be supported by solid and accurate research. Credibility is also established based on your communication techniques, both verbal and nonverbal.

Ernestine Sisneros, a guide at Salinas Pueblo Missions National Monument, New Mexico, is a direct descendant of the land grant family who settled here—this authenticity establishes credibility.

Tips to Enhance Credibility

▶ **Be prepared and organized.** The more you know about your topic, the better ready you are to deliver a smooth program and address questions from your audience beyond the scope of your presentation.

▶ **Dress professionally and appropriately.** First impressions are important for establishing credibility.

▶ **Be the authority.** Early in the program, establish your expertise on the topic by stating the source of your knowledge: experience, training, or research.

▶ **Reveal a personal connection with your topic.** This demonstrates that you have a stake in the topic and helps create a familiar relationship with the audience.

▶ **Be receptive.** An audience won't respond well to an interpreter who seems aloof or indifferent. An interpreter should show that they care and want to hear ideas and views from audience members.

▶ **Find common ground.** An audience will identify more easily with an interpreter if they perceive similarities and common interests.

▶ **Maintain eye contact. Use confident, clear, and vivid body language and words.** Your goal is to convince the audience that you are trustworthy and confident.

Overcoming Interference

This interpreter at Schmeeckle Reserve, Wisconsin, is reducing external interference by choosing a warm, sunny place to talk to the group and facing into the sun so the audience doesn't have to.

Interference is any factor that impedes the communication of a message. Interpreters working in public recreational settings combat multiple forms of interference on a daily basis. Reducing interference is essential for effective communication.

External interference includes environmental factors that are outside the realm of the interpreter or visitors. These might include a windy or rainy day for an outdoor talk, a hot or chilly room in the visitor center, noisy traffic near a road, or distracting groups of people participating in a recreational activity.

Internal interference refers to factors directly affecting audience members, including their basic needs, emotional state, or other internal distractions. A visitor might be hungry or need the restroom. Another might be itch-ing the poison ivy on her leg. Another might be thinking about which trail the family will hike the next day.

As an interpreter, your job is to first reduce the interference as much as possible, and then use communication techniques to combat the remaining interference.

Tips to Combat Interference

▶ **Minimize external distractions.** Choose areas away from noise and other activities. Stand so the sun and wind are in your eyes instead of in the visitors' eyes. Find shady places for hot days, or sheltered areas for windy days.

▶ **Minimize internal distractions.** Consider the visitors' basic needs; provide opportunities for rest and bathroom use.

▶ **Engage visitors.** Use sensory stimuli, stories, questions, and activities to keep their attention focused.

▶ **Be prepared.** Try to anticipate different conditions. For example, if you have a large crowd for a night hike, a colleague could be on call to assist so everyone experiences a quality program.

▶ **Have backup plans.** If unfavorable weather strikes, consider how you can adapt a program to be indoors or under shelter.

Distracted & Disruptive Visitors

Controversial topics, such as wolf reintroduction, can stir up strong emotions in some visitors who may disrupt a program.

Most audience members attending an interpretive program will be engaged, attentive, and supportive. Once in a while, however, you may encounter people who are distracted or disruptive. They may check text messages, talk to neighbors, ask purposely difficult questions, or challenge you personally.

The most important thing you can do in any situation is to stay in control, be calm, and convey a positive attitude. Don't take it personally. Unless they are disrupting other audience members, ignoring the distraction is often the best solution. The box below provides some tips for dealing with different types of disruptive audience members.

If a large number of your audience members are distracted, then perhaps it's time to liven up the presentation. Tell a story, make the audience laugh, use a different visual aid, ask a question, involve them, let them share a story with their neighbors, or have them stand up or sit down. These changes help refocus their attention on the program.

When an audience member asks a difficult question, just be honest. "I don't know" is always an acceptable answer. Never feel like you must know everything. Offer to assist them in looking up the answer after the program.

Types of Distracted and Disruptive Audience Members

Public speaking expert Diane DiResta describes several types of disruptive audience members:

▸ **Experts:** Know-it-alls who challenge your authority. Acknowledge comments without getting defensive. Invite and recognize their comments to make an ally.

▸ **Ramblers:** Storytellers who talk too much. Cut in politely, summarize the comments, and ask for other opinions.

▸ **Dominators:** Want control and intimidate a group by monopolizing the conversation. Don't let them take over. Ask for other responses.

▸ **Side Conversationalists:** Two or more people talk during your program. Make eye contact or stand in front of them until they stop speaking.

▸ **Complainers/Whiners:** Find fault with everything but have no solutions. Ask other audience members for alternatives. Stay focused and move on. You can't win!

▸ **Hecklers:** Disrupt program with unnecessary remarks. Best to ignore the person—trying a clever retort will challenge them to come back again.

Dealing with Hostile Individuals

A simple three-step method of dealing with hostile audience members is called Verbal Victories[SM]. The technique uses non-defensive conversation to prevent and diffuse potential conflicts. Professor Jon Hooper introduced this technique to the interpretive field.

Step 1: Collect More Information

Put yourself in the other person's shoes to see the world as they do. Ask the critic specific questions to clearly define what their question or statement means. Be neutral, non-judgmental, and non-defensive. Keep delving deeper to find the root cause of their disagreement. Rather than blaming or debating, this shows the person that you are genuinely interested in their concern and gives them a chance to vent.

> An audience member interrupts an interpreter during a talk about wolves.
>
> ---
>
> Visitor: "It's irresponsible of you to reintroduce wolves in this park!"
>
> Interpreter: "Can you explain your concern a bit more?"
>
> Visitor: "My neighbor raises cattle and he's worried about losing his calves to wolves. This is just a breeding ground for disaster."
>
> Interpreter: "Has your neighbor lost any calves to wolves recently?"
>
> Visitor: "He lost one a few years ago, but he knows others who lost calves this spring.

Step 2: Agree with the Critic

Find some way to agree with the critic. This "disarms" them. Disarming someone involves taking away their weapon—in this case, their hostility. The best way to accomplish this is to search for common ground. At minimum, agree that their viewpoint is understandable based on the information they have. By agreeing with a critic, you deflate their desire to fight back.

> Interpreter: "I grew up on a farm and I appreciate how costly and frustrating it is to see a healthy calf killed. A wolf that hunts livestock can become a real problem."

Step 3: Negotiate Differences

After empathizing and disarming, you finally share your point of view objectively. Be assertive yet tactful, with the aim of negotiating any remaining differences. Base your rationale on facts rather than feelings or beliefs. Use outside sources of information if possible to depersonalize the conversation.

> Visitor: "The wolves are a nuisance."
>
> Interpreter: "Wolves are an important part of a healthy ecosystem. Recent research by the U.S. Fish and Wildlife Service showed that less than 1% of cattle losses are due to wolves. Most die due to disease, digestive problems, and even weather."
>
> Visitor: "That doesn't help my neighbor stay in business."
>
> Interpreter: "If a wolf does take a calf, farmers can receive compensation from the government for their loss. I'd be happy to give you more information about this program after the talk. Today, we'll be focusing on the positive impacts that wolves have had here in the park."

References

Communication Process

▶ Fazio, J. R. & Gilbert, D. L. (2000). Public relations and communications for natural resource managers. Kendall/Hunt Publishing Co.: Dubuque, IA.

▶ Lucas, S. E. (2007). *The art of public speaking* (9th ed.). McGraw Hill: Boston, MA.

Nonverbal Communication

▶ Bizzell, P. & Herzberg, B. (Eds.) (2001). *The rhetorical tradition: Readings from classical times to the present* (2nd ed.). Beford/St. Martin's: Boston, MA.

▶ Hall, E. T. (1966). *The hidden dimension.* Doubleday: New York, NY.

▶ Knapp, M. L. & Hall, J. A. (2002). *Nonverbal communication in human interaction* (5th ed.). Thomson Learning, Inc.

▶ Pease, A. & Pease, B. (2006). *The definitive book of body language.* Bantam Dell: New York, NY.

▶ Wertheim, E. G. (2005). *The importance of effective communication.* Northeastern University. Retrieved from http://ysrinfo.files.wordpress.com/2012/06/effectivecommunication5.pdf

The Message

▶ Provost, G. (1972). *100 ways to improve your writing.* New American Library: New York, NY.

Multiple Intelligences

▶ Gardner, H. (2011). *Frames of mind: The theory of multiple intelligences* (3rd ed.). New York, NY: Basic Books.

Establishing Credibility

▶ Gass, R. H. & Seiter, J. S. (2007). *Persuasion, social influence, and compliance gaining* (3rd ed.). Pearson, Allyn and Bacon: Boston, MA.

Overcoming Interference

▶ Lucas, S. E. (2007). *The art of public speaking* (9th ed.). McGraw Hill: Boston, MA.

Distracted & Disruptive Visitors

▶ DiResta, D. (1998). *Knockout presentations: How to deliver your message with power, punch and pizzazz.* Worcester, MA: Chandler House Press.

▶ Hooper, J. (2014, October 15). Personal communication.

Image Citations

All photos copyright of the authors unless noted below.

- ▶ P. 74: Ranger Kelli English interpreting to a visitor, photo by Doug Moore
- ▶ P. 79: Diagram representation of personal space limits; courtesy of user WebHamster at Wikimedia Commons (CC BY-SA 3.0)
- ▶ P. 83: Pileated Woodpecker (6259355443); courtesy of user nigel at Flickr (CC BY 2.0)
- ▶ P. 89: Photo by Dennis Yockers

Website Resources
www.interphandbooks.org

Video Clips

- ▶ **Secrets of Body Language:** The science of non-verbal signals is revealed through this documentary produced by The History Channel.

- ▶ **The Importance of Being Inauthentic:** Communication expert Mark Bowden describes the importance of body language when making first impressions.

- ▶ **Multiple Intelligences:** Dr. Howard Gardner explains his theory of multiple intelligences.

- ▶ **Dealing with Hecklers:** David Shephard, a specialist in Neuro Linguistic Programming, discusses how to deal with hecklers.

5

Creative Interpretive Techniques

" *Good communication is just as stimulating as black coffee, and just as hard to sleep after.* Anne Morrow Lindbergh

Freeman Tilden wrote that "interpretation is an art" and knowledge should be treated "imaginatively." Good interpretation requires more than just presenting information. Successful interpreters use a diversity of creative techniques to reveal information in ways that relate to and inspire their audience members.

A character interpreter at Cabrillo National Monument, California, reveals the everyday life for keepers and their families in Old Point Loma Lighthouse.

Props/Visual Aids

An interpreter at the Sanibel-Captiva Conservation Foundation, Florida, invites visitors to touch a string of whelk egg cases found on the beach.

People pay attention to things they are curious about. A prop, or visual aid, is any physical item that is on stage with you or that you carry along—specimens, pictures, artifacts, models, tools, books, or even food. They focus attention and illustrate your messages. When revealed and used provocatively, props heighten curiosity and understanding.

Involve people's senses with props. We remember what we experience. A visitor who touches the soft plumage of an owl will appreciate its silent flight. If they hold an owl egg, they'll never forget its shape or color. An owl call captures attention and might even draw in a real owl. Opening a jar of skunk scent (and quickly closing it again!) memorably reveals that Great Horned Owls prey on skunks.

People respond to familiar objects when they are used in innovative ways. Such props help you draw analogies between common objects and the natural world. Assembling a flashlight—batteries, bulb, lens—clearly shows the concept of interdependence.

People are drawn to authentic objects, such as real mounts, skulls, or historical artifacts. Artifacts help create an atmosphere of a bygone era. Rolling a big log with an old cant hook or touching the button from the jacket of a Confederate soldier are ways of traveling through time.

Objects can also add to your credibility. Tools like a spotting scope or binoculars create an aura of expertise. Holding a ten-gauge shotgun while telling the story of the passenger pigeon adds authenticity to your tale. Quoting Thoreau from a frayed, yellow copy of *Walden* helps create an authentic atmosphere.

Participants at this "Late Bloomers" hike in Schmeeckle Reserve, Wisconsin, are encouraged to smell the leaves of fragrant plants.

 Watch Park Ranger Kevin Poe's use of props to interpret geology at Bryce Canyon National Park.

www.interphandbooks.org

The box below provides general tips for using props and visual aids. See page 126 for specific ideas about using props in interpretive talks, page 168 for using props in guided walks and tours, and page 181 for using props in spontaneous interpretive encounters.

Tips for Using Props/Visual Aids

▶ **The prop must be relevant to the theme.** To be effective, the prop must help support your main message in some way.

▶ **Organize your props.** Prior to your program, ensure that your props are organized and can be accessed quickly. If you have pictures, be sure they are in the right order.

▶ **Be sure all audience members can see each prop.** It's frustrating when audience members in the back can't see a prop. For larger groups, lift each prop above your head or set them on a high stand. If possible, walk through the audience so everyone can get a good look. For pictures, print them as large as possible.

▶ **Involve the senses.** For small groups, let people touch, smell, or, when appropriate, taste props for sensory involvement.

Passing around props is an excellent way for people to get an up-close look, but it does distract them from your program.

▶ **Keep the prop hidden until you need it.** This increases the impact of the prop when revealed and reduces distraction during your talk. When you are finished using it, put it away again.

▶ **Avoid talking to the prop.** A prop often serves as a crutch for speakers. Keep your attention focused on the audience.

▶ **Use creative props.** Consider what you are trying to illustrate and then find or make props to support the message. An outline of an alligator cut out of paper can dramatically show size. A gallon of water can demonstrate how much a black bear cub weighs.

A student interpreter at Schmeeckle Reserve, Wisconsin, involves the audience by inviting them to play several types of duck calls.

Humor

The use of humor can be a powerful communication technique. When used skillfully, it is inclusive and draws audiences into the talk. It relaxes listeners and helps break down barriers between audience members. A humorous story can make the interpreter more approachable and set the tone for the whole program.

One interpreter was presenting a campground program on how to build a campfire. He began by stating, "If one match is all it takes to burn down a forest, then why does it take a whole box to build a campfire?" His audience could easily relate to the frustration of struggling to start a fire. Even if the humorous statement didn't cause more than a smile or a chuckle, it introduced the subject in a light-hearted and unintimidating way.

Sometimes a humorous theme can be interwoven throughout a program, as was the case

Professor Sarah A. Brupt, a character at the San Diego Zoo in California, uses humor to share her quirky knowledge about zoo animals.

with an interpretive workshop conducted on St. Patrick's Day. The program began with a puff of smoke, a projected rainbow, and the surprise entry of a ridiculously attired leprechaun promising a pot of skills by the end. There was a talk on the history of the potato and a walk on shamrocks and wood sorrels. At the conclusion,

---

Tips for Using Humor

▶ **Relate humor to the talk theme.** Humor should only be used if it illustrates an important point about the subject. If used only for a laugh, it is inappropriate.

▶ **Use inoffensive humor that the audience can identify with.** Commonplace incidents can be humorous when seen from a new perspective. It is important to exercise good taste and not embarrass your audience. If anyone is a target of humor, make it you.

▶ **A humorous story or anecdote should arrive unannounced.** It should drift in and out of the plot as unobtrusively as Peter Parker, not as flamboyantly as Spider-Man.

▶ **Humor requires timing and delivery to be effective.** Use humor only if you feel comfortable with it and understand it. A successful interpretive program doesn't require humor.

each participant kissed the Blarney Stone before receiving their golden token pronouncing them a "certified guide." The lead leprechaun was confident, fun-loving, and unembarrassed, which created a safe environment for the participants to let go of their inhibitions and take chances in an interactive workshop.

Experience David Stokes' humorous and entertaining interpretation style.

www.interphandbooks.org

David Stokes, an entertaining naturalist and educator, uses live creatures, puppets, props, songs, and short stories to bring humor and fun into his presentations.

Isaac Ferris was a river pilot who in the late 1800s led crews floating lumber rafts down the Wisconsin River. Mike Gross, professor of interpretation, brings this character to life with the words, "I'm looking for some good men to raft lumber down this river. Are there any good men here?" The audience is engaged with humorous accounts of what life would be like for them on the river.

An interpreter at Schmeeckle Reserve, Wisconsin, dresses up an audience member as a frog to showcase adaptations, including a long sticky tongue and webbed toes. This involving technique elicits a humorous response from the audience while making the message memorable.

Questioning Techniques

Questioning provides opportunities for an audience to be engaged in an interpretive program. Instead of a one-sided lecture, questions create a two-way "interpretive conversation" that is more personal and meaningful for visitors.

Before your program starts, ask questions to learn about your audience, such as where they traveled from, if they have been to your site before, or what drew them to this particular program.

During the program, questioning strategies encourage involvement and gauge levels of understanding. Avoid simple yes-or-no type questions. Use a variety of question types with each having a purpose that relates to the theme. The quality, not the quantity, of questions is important.

Focus Questions

Focus questions ask the audience to describe, name, observe, or recall. They can help you structure a program and encourage involvement. However, they do not typically provoke creative thinking.

- ▶ "What have you heard about biofuels?"
- ▶ "What do you observe about the tracks along the trail?"
- ▶ "How many soldiers were killed during the American Civil War?"

This cultural interpreter at Heritage Hill State Park, Wisconsin, asks her group questions to involve them and to better determine their understanding of historical agricultural practices.

Process Questions

Process questions ask the audience to analyze, compare, explain, or group. They encourage people to integrate information rather than just remember or describe.

- ▶ "What would happen if wolves were removed from the ecological food chain?"
- ▶ "How do birds survive in the winter if they do not migrate?"
- ▶ "Why do the patterns etched into these indigenous pots differ from one another?"

Evaluation Questions

Evaluation questions challenge the audience to imagine, predict, theorize, or extrapolate. They deal with matters of value, judgment, and choices. They allow audience members to express their feelings.

- ▶ "What do you believe should be done about white-nose syndrome affecting bats?"

▸ "How would damming this river impact natural and human communities?"

▸ "What influences did the Lewis and Clark Expedition have on Native American cultures?"

Rhetorical Questions

Not all questions require a verbal response from visitors. **Rhetorical questions** are asked when you don't expect visitors to answer aloud. Involving and dramatic rhetorical questions help emphasize important points in a program.

For example, "If we can't solve the air pollution problem, what will become of our Northeastern forests? What will become of the pine and oak we depend on for our homes? What will we do when there are no more maple trees and syrup for our pancakes? What will happen to the plants and animals that depend on those trees for food, shelter, and protection?"

These questions don't demand an actual response, but they do involve the listener.

Hierarchy of Questioning Types

A series of question types assists the audience in understanding more complex ideas and concepts. Build from simple focus questions (recall) to process questions (integrate) to more thoughtful evaluation questions (values). Then, cycle back to start a new line of questioning.

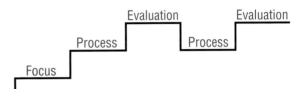

An example program on Lyme disease might use the following hierarchy:

1. Focus: "What do you know about the hosts of deer ticks?"

2. Process: "Based on your understanding of deer populations, why is Lyme disease on the rise?

3. Evaluation: "What do you believe should be done to reduce the number of Lyme disease incidents in the state?"

Tips for Questioning

▸ Direct most questions to the entire audience rather than a single individual. This indicates to the group that everyone is expected to think.

▸ Ask only one question at a time.

▸ Avoid asking questions that require only a simple yes or no (or a raise of hands).

▸ Allow time for an answer—this is called "wait-time." The longer a questioner allows for an answer, the better the answer will be. Never answer your own questions. If no one offers a response, rephrase the question or leave it open to be answered later.

▸ Do not start a question with, "Does anyone know…" or "Can anyone tell me…" Such phrases express doubt that the question can be answered.

▸ Pace questions to the ability of the group.

▸ Develop ideas and concepts through a series of questions. Build from focus questions to process questions to evaluation questions.

▸ Accept answers to questions gracefully, even if the answers are wrong. Never make someone feel foolish for participating in the program.

Storytelling

Ron Brown, a Grand Canyon National Park Ranger in Arizona, tells engaging stories about early explorers of the Colorado River.

> " *As a storyteller, your goal is to become, for a brief moment, something other than a man or woman standing in front of the room—to create a whole new world using words, sounds, gestures, and expressions. To hear a story is an ancient longing, to tell a story an ancient skill. A well-told story can move you to laughter or tears, it can explain or cause you to ponder the wonders of the universe.*
> Linda Yemoto and Simone Dangles

Storytelling is conveying events in words and images, engaging an audience's imagination to visualize, relate, and find meaning. When done effectively, storytelling is a powerful way to evoke emotion and interest in a topic. Oral storytelling is an age-old method of handing down history and passing along values.

Nearly every interpretive program has some storytelling component, whether sharing experiences from your own past, describing historical events, or conveying myths and legends.

According to naturalist and professional storyteller Linda Yemoto, storytelling is the "mother of all communication." Every culture

Tips for Storytelling

- ▶ Every good story describes some type of change to the character.

- ▶ Choose stories that mean something to you and that are relevant to your theme and program goals.

- ▶ Memorize a sequence of images for the story, not the words. Storytelling is most successful when presented in a conversational style with your own words. Avoid using notes. Memorize just the first line of your story, which gives you confidence when starting out and helps trigger the rest.

- ▶ Avoid using props since imagery is the storyteller's tool.

- ▶ Keep the listener's imagination engaged by using voice inflection that fits the action, gestures to paint images, sounds for dramatic effect, and distinct characters that interact.

- ▶ Use frequent pauses so the imagery can unfold, and use longer pauses to create suspense.

- ▶ Believe in yourself. If your body language lacks confidence, your audience will perceive it.

- ▶ Avoid talking in monotone, using a fake voice, talking too fast, insulting other cultures, and over-anthropomorphizing wildlife.

tells stories that connect to their history and teach values and morals. Storytelling bridges all forms of learning styles: visual, auditory, and kinesthetics (people feel something inside). When told as a story, information is more memorable and engaging.

Great storytelling is a special gift and an art that not everyone possesses. But anyone can learn to tell a *good* story. Storytellers have the ability to transport an audience to the scene being described and make them feel involved. It takes practice to sound natural, use appropriate gesturing, add well-timed pauses, and engage the audience through words.

Yemoto describes storytelling as equal parts art and science. The first part, story structure, is objective and can be taught and analyzed. At its simplest, stories have a beginning (set up), a middle (confrontation), and an end (resolution). More complex structures may include: exposition (setting forth meaning or purpose), rising action, climax, falling action, and denouement (final outcome).

The second part, character development, is more subjective. This includes everything that makes the story character believable to an audience: physical description, feelings, behavior, and personality traits.

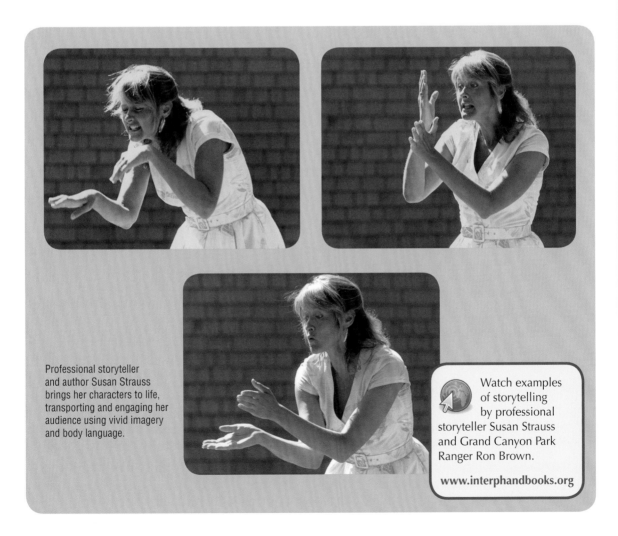

Professional storyteller and author Susan Strauss brings her characters to life, transporting and engaging her audience using vivid imagery and body language.

Watch examples of storytelling by professional storyteller Susan Strauss and Grand Canyon Park Ranger Ron Brown.

www.interphandbooks.org

Guided Imagery

Using guided imagery, a group is taken back to a time before farms while sitting in an Iowa prairie remnant.

Guided imagery, or visualization, asks audiences to take "mental field trips" to other places or times. Losing yourself in a relaxed state of imagination creates real physiological changes. In the medical profession, guided imagery is often used for stress relief. Athletes use guided imagery to prepare themselves mentally for their competition.

In the interpretive field, the presenter establishes a relaxing setting and guides the audience on an imaginary journey by describing what they are seeing, feeling, hearing, and smelling. This storytelling technique can be a powerful way to connect with people's emotions.

For example, an interpreter can take a group back to the Battle of the Little Bighorn, complete with the smell of gunpowder, the yelling of soldiers, and the heat of the sun on the open plain. You can explore endless places that may be too dangerous in real life, like a thunderstorm from atop a tree or the inside of an erupting volcano. Travel through space to see a supernova, swim to the bottom of an ocean, climb to the top of Mt. Everest, dig through the layers of the earth, or leap through time—guided imagery engages your audience's imagination.

Tips for Using Guided Imagery

▶ When developing the script for the journey, write down the sensory and visual images that you will share. Create specific images that relate to the audience's common experiences.

▶ Using descriptive language gets the fantasy trip started, and then each audience member's imagination takes over. Each has a unique journey.

▶ Be sure to research the subject well to create accurate images.

▶ Guided imagery is most effective when conducted with small groups.

▶ Place the audience in a peaceful, trusting place with minimal distractions where they will feel comfortable tapping into their imagination.

▶ Invite the audience to close their eyes or focus on a specific resource (flowing water, sky). This can reduce external distractions.

▶ Use good storytelling techniques to guide the group. Take time, use long pauses, and allow the audience to visualize the scene.

▶ If appropriate, ask group members to share their experiences after the journey. An interpreter can use these descriptions and emotions to support the theme of their presentation.

Guided Imagery Example: Human History on the Wisconsin River

The following script was used to help visitors imagine past life along the Wisconsin River. It sets the stage for character interpretation by a Jesuit priest.

"As you sit on these ancient granite rocks polished by ice and water, gaze into the dark current and drift back 10,000 years. Across the river, just out of view, stands a massive wall of ice, higher than the tallest tree and stretching for thousands of miles to the Arctic Circle. The water in the river runs milky green with powdered rock from the glacier.

"At the edge of the glacier, you see dark-haired people wearing animal skins surrounding a furry elephant-like creature. The mammoth trumpets as the people sling spears into its underbelly.

"The river drifts on through the centuries. The climate warms, the great ice sheets melt. The conical reflection of spruce trees in the river is replaced by the bright autumn glow of maple trees. A band of Winnebago people are making wigwams for their winter sugar camp.

"After the season of the popping trees, early spring to us, they tap the trees with bone drills and insert hollow sumac stems. Hot stones hiss as they are dropped into sap-filled holes in the ground that give off the sweet aroma of maple sugar. Children play noisily with snow snakes, carved sticks that they send skidding down ice-lined trenches. They laugh and happily talk in a tongue you do not understand.

"They stop abruptly and run excitedly to the water. Far upriver, drifting downstream, is a black-robed figure in a birch bark canoe, paddled by men of another tribe."

At this point, a black-robed Jesuit priest appears in a canoe singing in French. The fantasy trip ends and a characterization of Jesuit exploration on the Wisconsin River begins.

Jacques Marquette and Louis Joliet in canoe, with two other men, 1673.

Demonstrations

An interpreter demonstrates how to split slate by hand at the National Slate Museum in Wales, United Kingdom.

❝ Give a man a fish and he will eat for a day. Teach a man to fish and he will eat for the rest of his life. Ancient proverb

A demonstration is an interpretive technique that clearly shows your audience how something is done using authentic artifacts, tools, and objects. It combines narrative with action. Seeing a demonstration, and especially participating in it, leads to greater understanding.

Demonstrations are a core component of cultural history programs. They help visitors visualize past events and cultural traditions. Audience members may help churn butter, discover how a soldier fires a black powder musket, or taste maple syrup boiled from sap. Indigenous demonstrators at interpretive sites may showcase their craft, food, music, or dance traditions, helping keep their culture alive and thriving.

Recreation and survival-based programs offer prime opportunities for demonstrations.

Audience members can participate in pitching a tent, crafting snowshoes, setting a trap, or starting a fire by rubbing sticks together. In addition to discovering new information about a topic, visitors also gain new skills.

Natural history topics can also be enhanced through authentic demonstrations. Visitors can twist an increment borer into a tree and count the annual rings to age it, manipulate a radio telemetry antenna to track wildlife, or rattle antlers together to attract bucks during rut.

Tips for Demonstrations

▶ **Be sure that everyone in the audience can see the demonstration.** You may need to limit the group size for effective demonstrations.

▶ **Be prepared and practice.** Be sure that all components of the demonstration are organized and ready to be used. Practice beforehand to make sure the demonstration flows smoothly.

▶ **Encourage audience members to participate (if appropriate).** Hands-on activities create a memorable and meaningful experience for visitors.

▶ **Have enough supplies for everyone.** If you are presenting a candle-making demonstration, for example, be sure you have enough supplies for everyone in the group to make one.

Watch costumed interpreters demonstrate musket firing at Old Fort Niagara in New York.

www.interphandbooks.org

A costumed interpreter at Sleeping Bear Dunes National Lakeshore, Michigan, demonstrates the skills of those who once worked for the U.S. Life-Saving Service. Visitors help pull a volunteer's "body" from the frigid waters of Lake Michigan.

Children compete in a classic sack race at Heritage Hill State Historic Park, Wisconsin, to demonstrate early games.

An interpreter at the Vanuatu Cultural Center and National Museum on the island of Efate demonstrates the ancient tradition of sand-drawing, using only one finger that is never lifted.

Costumed Interpretation

A costumed interpreter assumes the appearance of a historic personality or a fanciful character. Characters engages the audience's imagination and evoke a wide range of emotions. They humanize events and make them real to visitors. Costumed interpreters choose from first-person (I/we), second-person (you), or third-person (he/she/they). Each has advantages and pitfalls.

First-person interpreter Shelton Johnson portrays Elizy Boman, a Buffalo Soldier from Troop K, Ninth U.S. Calvary, who in 1903 was assigned to protect Yosemite National Park, California.

First-Person Interpretation

A first-person costumed interpreter projects the persona of a historical figure or a character, speaking as if they were that person in that time period. The audience's imagination is engaged as they are swept away to another time or place.

▶ Theatrical skill makes the character believable.

▶ A plausible opening introduces the character and prepares the audience for the experience.

▶ The interpreter must stay in character to maintain the spell. A historic character would have no knowledge of modern-day events. However, the character should not embarrass visitors by questioning their "inappropriate" attire or engage in arguments based on the character's prejudices.

Second-Person Interpretation

Second-person interpretation engages visitors to participate in programming and activities. The character initiates a conversation with visitors as if all individuals existed in the same time period. Visitors pretend to be historical figures, even though they are not dressed in period costume. For example, at a "station" on the Underground Railroad, visitors assume the identity of runaway slaves. The costumed interpreter facilitates their experience so they can sense the fears and hopes in their journey to freedom.

▶ The interpreter poses questions that imply that visitors have entered the past: "I am told you were brought here in a wagon covered with straw. How did you feel about escaping?"

▶ A facilitator of second-person interpretation requires great skill in handling responses that aren't appropriate to the time period.

Third-Person Interpretation

Third-person interpreters wear costumes but act as themselves and treat visitors as a normal modern audience.

- ▶ Provides maximum flexibility. The interpreter can answer questions and develop a context outside the realm of the character.
- ▶ May be less intimidating to visitors.
- ▶ The costume serves as a prop, lending credibility to the information presented.

A costumed third-person interpreter at Heritage Hill State Park in Wisconsin invites visitors to participate in 18th-century activities.

Creating Authentic Characters

Shelton Johnson, a Yosemite National Park interpreter, developed a first-person character from old photos and historic accounts of the Buffalo Soldiers who were dispatched to Yosemite National Park in 1903. He assumed the name Elizy Boman, picked from the Yosemite muster rolls, but developed a character that is a composite of all of the 400 to 500 Buffalo Soldiers who served after the Civil War.

 Watch Shelton Johnson portray his Buffalo Soldier character, Elizy Boman, and discover how he developed it.

www.interphandbooks.org

Ways to Create Authentic Characters

- ▶ **Choose characters who would know about the time period or concepts to be interpreted.** Avoid famous personalities. For example, a visitor has preconceived notions about Eleanor Roosevelt. It is better to interpret through a minor participant, like Eleanor's secretary.

- ▶ **Develop individuals, not stereotypes.** Think of a character as a real individual with past experiences and inner motivations. When developing a character, ask the questions: Who am I? How do I sound? What mannerisms do I have? What is my background and temperament? How am I like the audience?

- ▶ **Attention to character detail is essential.** Clothing should be authentic to the character. It should not look like a costume but rather as something the character lives and works in.

- ▶ **Authentic props and tools add to the drama of any characterization.**

- ▶ **Small personal touches can put the final stamp of credibility on a character.** A pioneer woman must have hands that are rough with worn fingernails. A teamster should have leather-stained palms.

- ▶ **Think in terms of actions, not words.** A voyageur strains under a load of pelts and groans and grunts as he drops the pelts on the shore. Visualize the action and then portray it.

- ▶ **Stage dramatic entrances.** The character's first words and actions should capture the audience's attention.

Fanciful Characters

Costumed interpretation need not be limited to historical figures. Fanciful characters can lead us through worlds that can only be imagined. They can add personality to animals, plants, natural phenomena, or even inanimate objects such as rocks or chairs.

Schmeeckle Reserve in Wisconsin sponsors annual community festivals based on specific natural history themes. Visitors gather around a campfire where interpreters dressed as characters tell the story of their lives.

One program featured different spiders of the Reserve. Each interpreter selected a species to research and prepared a brief talk. Using common household items—like sponges, fabric, glue, Styrofoam, duct tape, spray paint, and chicken wire—they crafted characters for the show. The interpreters donned their costumes and assumed the personalities of their spider (how would a wolf spider act differently than a crab spider?).

As part of a "Storm Stories" program, interpreters at Schmeeckle Reserve, Wisconsin, portray characters who represent weather.

Another program highlighted storms. Characters included a depressed rain cloud, a lightning-wielding Zeus, a twirling tornado, and a hail-throwing baseball player.

The key to creating a successful fanciful character is to theatrically play up its personality. How would your character see the world that humans are living in? Exaggerated gestures, body movements, and inflection create a dramatic aura that brings the character to life.

 Watch interpreters bring fanciful characters to life at the "Web of Life" and "Storm Stories" campfire programs.

www.interphandbooks.org

"Goldie" the crab spider demonstrates how she hunts for prey.

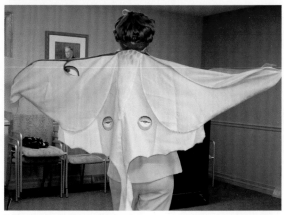

A "luna moth" shows off her wings.

Live Animal Programs

The confidence and behavior of the interpreter/handler is important to both the animal and the audience, as demonstrated by this educator at the Raptor Education Group, Inc. (REGI) in Wisconsin. Invest in developing a solid rapport with your animal partner.

Animals add a dynamic and unpredictable air of excitement to interpretive programs, which attracts and holds the attention of audiences. We all like to meet other living creatures and watch them up close. Live animals can be the door to a greater appreciation and understanding of ecological concepts.

Live animal programs require careful planning to be successful, safe, and trouble-free. The animal's well-being should be paramount and obvious to the audience. The proper permits must be obtained and all wildlife laws must be obeyed. Handlers must be extremely comfortable with the animal and be prepared for unexpected events like defecation, wing flapping, and defensive behavior. Ideally, the interpreters should also be the animals' caretakers to ensure that they have a comfortable relationship with the creature. Some species are better suited to the stress of interacting with audiences and some individuals have a higher tolerance of being handled.

Animals in the Wild

Animals don't have to be captive to take part in a program. Feeding stations can serve as center stage for interpreting the behaviors of birds, squirrels, and chipmunks. Serendipitous encounters with frogs, snakes, crayfish, songbirds, or foxes out on the trail serve as exciting, unique, and memorable experiences for visitors.

An interpreter at Schmeeckle Reserve, Wisconsin, demonstrates the unique adaptations of snapping turtles.

 Watch a live animal program featuring owls by an educator at the Raptor Education Group, Inc.

Discover how live animals are used as part of the Minnesota Zoo's Zoomobile program that travels to schools and community events.

www.interphandbooks.org

Consider the wildlife opportunities at your site. Audiences are fascinated by witnessing the American Woodcock spring courtship flight at sunset, listening to the deafening chorus of frogs and toads, or watching the massive migrations of Canada Geese or Sandhill Cranes.

At Cabrillo Marine Aquarium in California, crowds gather on the beach to experience the famous grunion runs—tiny fish ride the breaking waves of high tide onto the beach to spawn and deposit eggs. Program staff engage the audience as they experience this phenomenal natural event.

Don't overlook the scores of potential tiny performers like ant lions, butterflies, earthworms, and critters that live under logs. They can be dynamic educators when they are put on stage. Clear plastic boxes serve as temporarily houses and invite safe handling and easy observation.

Traveling Animal Shows

Wildlife rehabilitation and nature centers often take live animal programs on the road to schools and other public facilities. These popular programs are ideal opportunities for educating about natural behavior and the role of animals in the wild. They present some challenges that interpreters should be prepared for.

Judy Armstrong, a naturalist with the Minnesota Zoo's Zoomobile, offers these suggestions for working with animals on the road:

▶ Be sure the animals feel safe and secure during transit.

▶ Prepare the audience by telling them to be quiet, sit still, and informing them of behaviors the animals might display (make noise, pace, stay on table, flap, defecate).

Program participants at Cabrillo Marine Aquarium, California, swirl sand and seawater in a baby food jar to stimulate grunion fish to burst out of their egg sacs.

▶ Look around the space for things that might distract the animal, such as balloons, artwork, or aquarium animals.

▶ Set yourself up so a wall or barrier is behind you and the animal is only viewable from the front—this makes the animal more comfortable (not surrounded).

▶ Tell a story about the animal so the audience relates—where it came from, how it was cared for, and why it has a name.

▶ Decide in advance whether the audience will be allowed to touch the animal. If so, establish rules for safe handling and identify handwashing stations.

Naturalist Judy Armstrong of the Minnesota Zoo's Zoomobile shares an armadillo with students in a classroom.

When animals are on display, such as this touch tank at the South Carolina Aquarium, a trained handler should be available to guide the visitor's interactions with the animals. Most program animals need resting periods away from the public.

Living history farms and historic sites, like Shaker Village of Pleasant Hill, Kentucky, gain authenticity and "come alive" by featuring livestock of the time period.

Tips for Live Animal Programs

▶ **Set expectations for audience behavior and respect for the animal before it arrives on stage.**

▶ **Never endanger an animal's health or well-being.** Audience handling of the animal should be limited. The interpreter should control the animal. If it shows stress, stop.

▶ **Live animals will attract the audience's full attention when they are out, often at the expense of your interpretive message.** Carefully consider when and how long to show an animal as part of your presentation. When it is not needed, put it in a safe, hidden area so the audience can return their attention to you.

▶ **Emphasize the fact that wild animals require special care and are not pets.** Explain why they have been removed from the wild.

▶ **Protect people from harm from the animals.**

▶ **Prepare for the unexpected.**

▶ **Avoid humanizing animals, such as using pet names or training them to do human activities.** This creates misconceptions about their role in the wild.

▶ **Demonstrate and explain natural animal behaviors.**

▶ **Don't limit yourself to interpreting only the large, showy creatures.** Include insects, amphibians, reptiles, crustaceans, and other small creatures. They are often easier to care for and can be captured short-term and then released.

▶ **Involve the audience in discovering wild animals in their native habitats.** Instead of just showing an animal as part of your program, have the audience help in finding and contributing to the study of wildlife species. Examples of these programs include bird and bat banding stations, amphibian and reptile population counts, wildlife feeding stations, butterfly-watching hikes, sea turtle nesting programs, and birdhouse monitoring.

Music, Movement, and Sound

An interpreter at the Vanuatu Cultural Center and National Museum on the island of Efate plays a traditional tune on a wooden flute, lending an authentic ambience to the cultural program.

Music is in our blood. The rhythmic pulse of life is evident in sounds of nature and history. Tones, rhythms, and lyrics make us happy, sad, attentive, or relaxed. Music, in its diverse forms of sound and song, is a powerful communication tool. Music and movement connect with an array of different learning styles, and the kinesthetic experience creates lasting memories.

You don't have to be a talented soloist or genius songwriter to effectively use music in your program. If you can play an instrument or you enjoy singing, then definitely consider how concepts can be revealed through song.

A pair of Forest Service interpreters in Alaska livened up their talk on salmon reproduction by pulling out a guitar and singing "Bring back, bring back, oh bring back my sockeye to me, to me!" as a parody of the well-known "My Bonnie Lies Over the Ocean." It and other parodies became audience favorites, and visitors requested to see "The Singing Rangers" as soon as they arrived at the visitor center.

Involve the audience through music and movement. Teach them a simple chorus that they can sing with you. Give them instruments to play. Encourage them to clap their hands or stomp their feet. Invite them to use hand gestures to visually represent the song's words.

Music is more than just song. Simple rhythm and movement can be subtly interwoven with other techniques to create a richer and more involving experience.

A wetland symphony can be created with audience members playing homemade instruments that simulate the calls of various frogs, birds, and insects. Once participants run their thumb down the teeth of a comb or pluck a loose rubber band, they'll always remember what a chorus frog or green frog sounds like.

If you are less musically inclined, incorporating recorded music and sounds into a program can still be a powerful connector. Playing quiet background music, for example, helps set the stage for an experience like a historic presentation or a visual journey into space.

Watch Tom Pease perform several of his fun and involving songs.

www.interphandbooks.org

Tom Pease is a children's performer who uses song, movement, sign language, and humor to interpret concepts to his audiences. According to Tom, "Besides the fact it's a blast, the use of song in teaching simply helps open up a child's mind to the subject at hand. Melody and rhyme often give them other ways of remembering a lesson."

Tips for Using Sounds, Rhythm, and Music in Your Programs

▶ Use familiar tunes and add lyrics to create songs that are thematic to your program.

▶ Add sound effects and background music appropriate to your subject and theme.

▶ Plan for audience participation by using rhythm, movement, and sound like clapping, drumming, stomping, pantomime, etc.

▶ Use a projector or hand out copies of lyrics when you encourage sing-alongs.

▶ Recruit assistants from the audience to help lead songs, skits, and body movements.

▶ Be enthusiastic and exude confidence and fun.

References

Props/Visual Aids

▶ Zimmer, J. (2011, September 29). Ten Tips for Using Props in a Presentation. *Manner of Speaking Blog*. Retrieved from http://mannerofspeaking.org/2011/09/29/ten-tips-for-using-props-in-a-presentation/

Storytelling

▶ Yemoto, L. (2011). Don't be such a scientist: science versus storytelling. (Presentation for NAI National Workshop, Saint Paul, Minnesota). *2011 Interpretive Sourcebook* and notes: National Association for Interpretation.

▶ Yemoto, L. & Dangles, S. (1980). *Storytelling—Be a better bard*. Unpublished handout: Berkeley, CA.

Demonstrations

▶ Hughes, C. (1998). *Museum theatre: Communicating with visitors through drama*. Heinemann Publishing: Portsmouth, NH.

Costumed Interpretation

▶ Hughes, C. (1998). *Museum theatre: Communicating with visitors through drama*. Heinemann Publishing: Portsmouth, NH.

▶ Magelssen, S. (2006, May). Making history in the second person: post-touristic considerations for living historical interpretation. *Theatre Journal 58*(2), 298–304.

Live Animal Programs

▶ Armstrong, J. (2014, December 18). Personal communication.

Music, Movement, and Sound

▶ Pease, T. (2014, December 4). Personal communication.

Image Citations

All photos copyright of the authors unless noted below.

▶ P. 97: David Stokes photo courtesy of David Stokes

▶ P. 97: Isaac Ferris river pilot photo courtesy of Doug Moore

▶ P. 100: Ranger Ron Brown photo courtesy of Grand Canyon National Park

▶ P. 101: Susan Strauss photo series courtesy of Diane Kulpinski

▶ P. 103: [Jacques Marquette and Louis Joliet in canoe, with two other men, 1673]. By Edgar S. Cameron, circa 1911. Library of Congress, Miscellaneous Items in High Demand Collection, [LC-USZ62-116498]

▶ P. 105: Sleeping Bear Dunes National Lakeshore demonstration photo courtesy of Dennis Yockers

▶ P. 106: Shelton Johnson photo by Tami A. Heilemann, U.S. Department of the Interior

- P. 109: Interpreter with owl photo courtesy of the Raptor Education Group, Inc.
- P. 110: Armadillo program photo courtesy of Judy Armstrong, Minnesota Zoo
- P. 111: Shaker Village of Pleasant Hill photo courtesy of Megan Espe
- P. 113: Tom Pease photo courtesy of Tom Pease

Website Resources
www.interphandbooks.org

Video Clips

- **Kevin Poe—Using props:** Ranger Kevin Poe uses props, humor, visual aids, and multiple perspectives to interpret geology and global climate change at Bryce Canyon National Park.

- **David Stokes—Using humor:** Naturalist and educator David Stokes demonstrates his humorous interpretation style through the use of songs, live animals, costumes, puppets, props, and movement.

- **Susan Strauss—Storytelling:** Professional storyteller Susan Strauss shares a variety of stories with audiences.

- **Ron Brown—Storytelling:** Grand Canyon National Park Ranger Ron Brown tells engaging stories about early explorers of the Colorado River.

- **Demonstration example:** Costumed interpreter soldiers at Old Fort Niagara in New York interpret and demonstrate musket firing.

- **Shelton Johnson—Buffalo Soldier character interpretation:** Yosemite National Park Ranger Shelton Johnson portrays his Buffalo Soldier character, Elizy Boman, and describes how he developed it.

- **Leslie Goddard—Creating historically authentic characters:** Historical interpreter Leslie Goddard describes tips for researching and developing authentic characters.

- **Fanciful character interpretation:** Student interpreters at Schmeeckle Reserve, Wisconsin, bring fanciful characters to life at the "Web of Life" and "Storm Stories" campfire programs.

- **Live animal program example:** An educator at the Raptor Education Group, Inc. (REGI) in Wisconsin presents a program with live owls.

- **Minnesota Zoo Zoomobile programs:** Discover how the Minnesota Zoomobile program offers outreach to schools and other organizations using live animals.

- **Tom Pease—Music, sound, and movement:** Children's performer and educator Tom Pease performs several of his fun, humorous, and engaging songs.

6

Interpretive Talks

❝ *Let thy speech be better than silence, or be silent.*
Dionysisus the Elder

Talks are at the heart of all interpretive programs. Well planned and orchestrated talks have the power to enthrall audiences and guide them on engaging adventures of discovery. An effective interpretive talk is far more than well-chosen words. People's senses should be stimulated by sounds, smells, sights, and touch. Their intellectual curiosity should be piqued to the point that they are eager to learn more.

An interpreter leads a talk at the Aldo Leopold Shack and Farm, Wisconsin.

Interpretive Talk Basics

Talks are the fundamental tool of interpreters. Interpreters give talks at visitor centers, amphitheaters, campfires, and major site attractions. Talks are also presented off-site at schools, service club meetings, workshops, and other venues.

Interpretive talks are defined by an interpreter addressing a more-or-less stationary audience, in contrast to a guided walk or tour, where the audience moves from one place to another. For short talks (5 minutes or less), the group typically stands. For longer presentations, seating should be made available.

Talks take on many forms and functions. Interpreters give orientation programs, discuss specific natural and cultural resources, demonstrate skills and trades, present multimedia programs, use props, portray characters, and tell stories.

Benefits and Challenges

Talks have several benefits when compared to walks or tours:

- The gathering space can be set up as needed before the program begins.
- Nearly anyone can attend talks, even those with mobility impairments.
- With preparation, large groups can be handled much more effectively than in a guided walk or tour.
- Talks are ideal for showing props or using

An interpreter dons a chef hat to describe the ingredients of ecological change in Rocky Mountain National Park, Colorado.

audiovisual technology since the interpreter is "on stage."
- External interference, such as temperature, weather, and noise, can be better controlled in an indoor environment.

Talks also have some challenges, especially when dealing with large groups:

- Visitors in the back may have trouble seeing the presenter and props. A tiered seating area (like an amphitheater) or a raised stage is essential for large groups.
- People may have issues hearing the presenter, especially in outdoor settings. A microphone and speaker system may be necessary.
- Unlike guided walks, talks often interpret resources that aren't immediately on hand to experience—they require extra interpretive effort to be meaningful.

Tips for Giving Effective Interpretive Talks

▶ **Be prepared.** Preparation is critical for credibility. Know the resources and their importance. Understand your visitors' needs and interests. Recognize your management goals and objectives.

▶ **Plan by using an outline**. Start by developing an outline rather than writing out an entire script. Limit memorization to the introduction, body outline, transitions, and concluding statement.

▶ **Practice.** Practice out loud with friends or family using actual visual aids to build confidence. Record and watch your rehearsal to evaluate your program.

▶ **Make a good first impression.** Dress appropriately, one step up from your audience, and convey confidence. Avoid sunglasses or other barriers.

▶ **Be a good host.** Arrive early to greet visitors and interact. Be sure all visual aids are organized and prepared prior to starting the program. Provide seating for long programs.

▶ **Refrain from using notes.** Do not read from a script or use note cards—they prevent you from making eye contact and gesturing, and stifle your conversational tone and flow.

▶ **Structure your program around a theme.** An effective talk has a provocative introduction (POW!), a bridge (introduce yourself and theme), a body (with two to four subthemes), and an inspiring conclusion. These components are tied together by a focused theme.

▶ **Use visual and multisensory aids.** Props, pictures, drawing tools, projectors, audio gadgets, and multimedia tools help maintain interest and support your messages.

▶ **Use a variety of interpretive techniques.** Developing fresh approaches to your program will enhance its quality and effectiveness. Humor, questioning, sensory activities, and provocative examples involve the audience and meet the needs of multiple learning styles.

For interpretive talks with large audiences, a tiered seating area, like this stone amphitheater in Schmeeckle Reserve, Wisconsin, ensures that everyone has a clear view of the interpreter.

Structure Your Talk

Like a loud sound, a POW! catches the audience's attention by creatively revealing the topic. Costumed interpreters at Castillo De San Marcos National Monument, Florida, demonstrate a literal POW!

Once you have developed a specific program theme (see Chapter 3), it is time to build your actual presentation. An effective interpretive talk is like a good story—it has a beginning, a middle, and an end. The basic structure of a talk has five parts:

Basic Structure of Talk

▶ **POW!** Capture the group's attention with a provocative introduction.

▶ **Bridge.** Introduce yourself, establish credibility, and link to the theme.

▶ **Body.** Illustrate each subtheme of your program with examples and creative techniques.

▶ **Transitions.** Move smoothly from one subtheme to the next.

▶ **Inspiring Conclusion.** Conclude by presenting an inspiring call to action or message. Link back to the POW!

POW! Grab Their Attention

To start a program, you need to catch your audience's attention. An effective talk starts with a **POW!** When we hear a loud sound, our attention is automatically drawn to it. A provocative talk introduction does the same thing—it draws in the audience and promises a rewarding experience. It stokes their curiosity and interest.

An attention-grabbing introduction doesn't have to be loud. It just needs to creatively reveal your topic in an intriguing way.

Some example POW! techniques include:

▶ Asking the audience a thought-provoking question

▶ Leading the audience with guided imagery

▶ Playing sounds

▶ Reciting a poem or quote

▶ Involving the audience with a look, listen, or taste activity

▶ Telling a story

▶ Showing a dramatic image

▶ Pulling out an interesting prop

▶ Using a creative or unexpected metaphor

What catches a person's attention? Psychologist David G. Myers found that the following stimuli work best at attracting attention:

▶ Extreme stimuli, like very large, colorful, loud, or smelly things

▶ Movement and contrast

▶ Unexpected, novel, and surprising things

▶ Other living things (people, animals)

▶ Things connected to us

These ideas can be used to develop a fun, creative, and intriguing start to your program.

Bridge: Link to the Theme

Once you have captured the audience's attention with a creative POW!, you need to link it directly to your program theme and messages. The **Bridge** answers the questions, "Why was that said?" and "What does it mean to me?" It connects the beginning of the talk to the body, provides a formal introduction to you as a speaker, and reveals the focused theme that organizes the rest of the program. It provides a sense of direction for the audience.

Within the Bridge of the talk, you should:

▶ Welcome the visitors
▶ Introduce yourself
▶ Establish credibility: describe your background, experience, passion for the topic
▶ Introduce your theme (not necessarily word for word, but the audience needs to know what the talk is about)
▶ Introduce the main points of the talk
▶ Be enthusiastic and sincere

Examples of POW! and Bridge

Here are a couple of POW! and Bridge examples for an interpretive talk about loon communication. Which is most effective for the audience?

Example 1

"Hello, everyone. My name is Emily and I'm a naturalist here at the park. I've worked here for two years so I know this area very well. This evening we'll be talking about loons."

In this example the naturalist uses a fairly traditional and common approach. While she greets the audience and introduces herself, she doesn't have a strong POW! for capturing the audience's attention or interest. The general topic of loons is introduced, but the audience doesn't know specifically what the talk will cover.

Example 2

(Program begins with the naturalist playing a recording of an echoing loon call).

"That's a pretty eerie sound. You can probably understand why early settlers here thought the lake was haunted. Has anyone heard this sound before? It's actually the sound of a bird, and if we're not too loud, we'll probably hear a real one tonight. . . Hello, everyone. My name is Emily and I'm a naturalist here at the park. Over the past two years, I've heard, observed, and studied the loons that nest on our lake. Why do they make such crazy sounds? This evening, we'll discover the four distinct calls that loons make to communicate with each other."

In this example, the naturalist uses sound to grab the audience's attention, add a level of intrigue, and reveal the topic. She establishes her credibility by making it specific to the topic. And she introduces her focused theme of "loon communication" to better prepare the audience.

Body: Illustrate Your Subthemes

Your talk is based on a theme, the main idea you want your audience to absorb and remember. To share this effectively with the audience, you need to break your theme down into specific "chunks" that you can illustrate in the **Body** of your talk. These "chunks" are called subthemes. They provide the organizational structure of your talk.

Research has shown that people can remember only a limited amount of new information. Psychologist Nelson Cowan found that people best understand and remember new information when it is in four or fewer "chunks." Break down your main theme into **two to four specific subthemes** that you hope your audience will remember after the program.

Like the main theme, subthemes should do more that just list factual information. They should connect tangible resources with intan-

Kevin Stonerock, an interpretive performer and songwriter, portrays Ohio River steamboat captain Ebenezer Cline.

gible meanings in a way that the audience can relate to.

To be effective, every major idea must be illustrated in some way. Use visual aids such as props, pictures, or multisensory devices. Create mental images through metaphors and analogies, guided imagery, or storytelling. Involve the audience physically and relate to their experience.

Example of Developing Subthemes and Techniques

A program has the following theme: **"The livelihood of a Mississippi River riverboat pilot depended on his intimate knowledge of the river and its hazards."** You could share countless messages based on this, but people can only remember about two to four chunks of information. The following examples list potential subthemes and techniques for illustrating each.

Example 1: Focus on navigation
▶ Riverboat pilots needed to accurately measure the depth of the river (audience measures depth with sounding line)

▶ Pilots needed to know how the river was changing its course (tell story from Mark Twain, show map of river over time)

▶ Pilots needed to alert other boats of their presence in the dark or fog (play recordings of different whistles and what they mean)

Example 2: Focus on disasters
▶ Steamboat boilers could explode with disastrous results (play sound of an explosion, share story of *Sultana*, show pictures of the disaster)

▶ Submerged hidden snags could sink a steamboat (share story of *Arabia*, demonstrate using model of boat and snag)

▶ Unexpected violent storms could capsize a steamboat (share journal entry of survivor on *Hornet*)

Transitions: Moving From Subtheme to Subtheme

A **Transition** is something that indicates when an interpreter has finished one main idea and is moving on to another. Transitions are essential for the audience to understand the overall direction and organization of your program. They explain how one subtheme is linked to another.

The following sentences include transitional phrases that are underlined. Notice how they first remind the audience of the subtheme just completed before revealing the subtheme about to be discussed.

- "Now that we've discussed the way adult bears teach their young to open dumpsters, let's explore how we can prevent bears from eating our human food."
- "Keeping in mind the different ways that invasive species are introduced, let's return to our first point about the use of native plants in our yards."

Effective transitions are also conveyed through nonverbal communication. A pause allows time for the audience to think about what was just said. A shift in your movement (start walking if you had stopped for a while or vice versa), a planned gesture, or a change in your posture can all indicate that your program is transitioning to a new idea.

Beyond the words and body language, consider adding creative transitions that support the style of your talk. Humorous presentations could use a related amusing story to transition between each subtheme. A thought-provoking presentation could offer a rhetorical question at each transition. Each subtheme could be introduced with a story, a quote, a poem, or a picture.

Above all, when planning for your program, clearly define the transitions you will use. Well planned transitions are essential for an organized and professional talk.

Examples of Effective Transitions

- **Bridge words or phrases:** First, before, now, after, then, next, furthermore, meanwhile, in addition, consequently, as a result, on the other hand, nevertheless.

- **Flashback:** Remind the audience of a related message you already mentioned to introduce a new point.

- **Ask a question:** "How many of you...?" This involves the audience and encourages thinking.

- **Use humor:** Only if you feel comfortable and it fits the style of the presentation.

- **Use a visual or multisensory aid:** Intriguing artifacts, objects, pictures, cartoons, sounds, or music focus the audience's attention.

- **Pause:** A short silence creates a break in the presentation and allows time for the audience to think.

- **Use physical movement:** Plan an obvious change of location, gestures, posture, and/or facial expression.

- **Tell a personal story:** A brief anecdote reinforces points made and transitions to the new material.

Conclusion: Be Inspiring

The **Conclusion** of your talk tells the listener that you are done. In its most basic form, the conclusion is a summary that provides an opportunity to restate the theme and subthemes of the interpretive talk. But as interpreters, we can do better than that! Be as creative with the conclusion as you were for the POW! introduction.

Think of the ending as an inspirational close to the program that plants a seed in the visitors' minds. Avoid announcing a conclusion with dry language like, "To summarize . . ." or "In conclusion . . . ." Leave the audience wanting more and encourage them to discover on their own. Give them a call to action. Answer the question "So what?" An effective ending might be an inspiring quote, a dramatic story, or lingering music. Be sure to provide a clear ending statement so your audience is sure the program is over.

Professor and author Sam Ham recommends developing the parts of the program in a certain order—first develop the body (your main content and the storyline), then the conclusion, then the introduction. He describes this as the **2-3-1 rule**. You can't write a strong introduction for a program before knowing the details of the content in the body.

Examples of Conclusions

Here are a couple of conclusion examples for an interpretive talk about seed dispersal. Which is most effective for the audience?

Example 1

"To summarize, plants use several different methods to disperse their seeds—by animals, by wind, and by water. Thank you for coming today and I hope you enjoy your stay."

In this example the interpreter uses a standard, low-impact conclusion. He does thank the audience for coming and offers an obvious end to the program.

Example 2

"Despite being rooted in the ground, plants have evolved in an incredible variety of ways to spread their kind. Seeds blow in the wind. They float in the water. And they attach themselves to you and me. As Henry David Thoreau once wrote, 'Though I do not believe that a plant will spring up where no seed has been, I have great faith in a seed. Convince me that you have a seed there, and I am prepared to expect wonders.' I encourage you to go out and experience the wonder of seeds during your stay. Thank you for coming!"

The interpreter here relates the main points of the talk to his audience. He shares an inspirational quote. And he gives a call to action, encouraging the audience to look for seeds.

Effective Talk Presentation Techniques

Once you have outlined the structure of your talk, you can focus on how to present those messages to your audience. A variety of techniques will help make your interpretive talk a success.

Interacting with your audience before your talk is an important way to gain credibility and build confidence.

Setting the Stage

You begin communicating with your audience long before you utter your first words. Your grooming speaks about your dependability. Your posture states your competence. Your clothing shouts your credibility on the subject.

Be appropriately groomed and dressed with an alert, confident posture. Let your appearance assure the audience that you are competent—don't let them wonder if you are.

Be a good host. Arrive before your audience so you have time to ready equipment, prepare props, and check that everything is set for your guests.

By the time the first visitors arrive, you should be ready to make as many acquaintances as possible. Your warmth can melt barriers that exist between strangers. Gather some insights about your audience prior to your talk. One naturalist discovered he had a doctor from a poison center at his edible wild foods talk. This doctor added enlightening anecdotes from his experience when poisonous plants were shown.

Many audience members may have something to share that relates to your topic. A rancher has unique perspectives on prairies. A language teacher has a particular interest in the root meaning of plant names.

Come prepared. You should know your subject so well that you can concentrate on your delivery and respond to your audience.

Your Beginning

The first 30 seconds of your talk are critical to establishing rapport. Project warmth, confidence, and competence. Stand, smile, and use eye-to-eye contact. To do this, you must feel prepared. You should have practiced your talk so it flows easily.

Don't put up barriers between you and your audience, such as standing behind a podium or table. Be casual but not sloppy. Don't sit down, lean on an object, or put your hands in your pockets.

Visual and Multisensory Aids

Visual aids are fundamental tools of interpretive talks. Unlike guided walks and tours where the site itself is on stage, talks often require us to show tangible examples that transform words and abstractions into concrete, understandable ideas. They serve as authentic artifacts and specimens, metaphors and analogies, demonstrations, focal points, and even humorous distractions. The following section introduces common types of visual and multisensory aids that you might use in a talk.

Physical props, like this twig basket frame, enhance understanding and encourage sensory involvement.

Props/Objects

These are tangible objects that people can experience with their senses. They include artifacts, specimens, models, books, experiments, tools, and costumes. See page 94 for general tips about using props. A few additional guidelines:

- ▶ Use of props can be active or passive—you can either show a prop or pass it around.

- Passing objects can lead to distraction, so this is often better suited to small groups.
- ▶ Talk to the audience, not the prop.
- ▶ Hold props high so everyone can see. If possible, walk into the audience so people can see the object up-close.

General Guidelines for Using Visual Aids

- ▶ **Keep them simple and legible.** Use a greater number of simple visuals rather than a few complex ones. Make images and words large enough to be legible from the back of the group. Two to three-inch high letters are needed at a 15-foot viewing distance.

- ▶ **Make them look neat and professional.** This increases your credibility. It is better to enlarge a computer printout than to show a poorly rendered drawing or handwriting.

- ▶ **Be conservative.** Choose readable, familiar typefaces. Reserve capitals for titles only. Use complementary colors.

- ▶ **Relate visuals to spoken words.** Remember, they support and illustrate your ideas.

- ▶ **Show a visual aid only as long as it continues to provide relevant information.** Hide it or put it off to the side when not in use.

- ▶ **Avoid referring to the visual aid.** Expound upon what people can already see. Avoid saying "this is a…", "here is a…", etc.

- ▶ **Use a variety of visual aids.** This maintains audience interest and connects to different learning styles.

- When pointing to something, be slow and deliberate. Use a pointer to enhance audience focus.
- Whenever possible, involve the audience. Use additional senses. Invite someone up front to hold the prop.
- Rehearse how you will use your props. Plan the moment you will reveal them. There is a transition when each prop is introduced—plan this out to avoid disrupting the flow.

Pictures/Illustrations

The adage "a picture is worth a thousand words" is especially true for interpretive presentations. Photographs, drawings, posters, maps, diagrams, graphs, and charts can visually convey a large amount of meaning. Many of the guidelines for props also apply to pictures.

Some additional tips:
- Be sure the pictures are high quality and pertinent to the theme.

- Pictures need to be enlarged so the audience can see them. The larger the audience, the larger the picture size. For printed pictures, use at least tabloid (11" x 17") size paper.
- Hold pictures high and take them close to the audience.
- Pictures can be projected with an overhead projector, slide projector, or digital projector to ensure everyone can see. Keep images up only as long as you need them.
- An illustrated talk is a specific type of program that uses projected pictures to tell a story. Read the Illustrated Talk section starting on page 137 for recommendations.
- Always talk to the audience, not the picture.
- Don't make your talk a photo album. Limit the number of pictures that you show. Find other props or objects and use different techniques to illustrate your main points.

An interpreter describes the watertight properties of white oak using a visual of a sailing vessel.

Writing/Drawing Tools

Interpreters often give presentations in places without electricity. Chalkboards, whiteboards, and flip charts are low-tech and involving ways to show visuals that support your talk.

▶ Put extensive drawings or writing on the board or paper before your presentation begins. Taking too much time to write or draw creates restlessness.

▶ Don't talk to the board or paper. Eye contact with the audience is important!

▶ Avoid blocking the audience's view.

▶ If you need to add something during the presentation, don't talk while your back is turned to the audience. Pause your talk, quickly add your mark, and then turn back to the audience and continue talking.

▶ Plan ways to add meaningful details to the board or flip chart during your program. This infuses an element of spontaneity.

▶ Use marking pens with high contrast.

▶ Use colored markers for emphasis, but don't overuse them.

Interpreters at Spring Mountains National Recreation Area, Nevada, use a flip chart to illustrate the different parts of a flower.

▶ For flip charts, reveal sheets only when you are ready to discuss them.

▶ Vary your presentation techniques. Do not overuse or rely entirely on the board. Use props and other media during your presentation when appropriate.

Projection Tools

For presentation spaces with electricity, document cameras, overhead projectors, microscope projectors, and similar devices allow you to share small visuals by projecting enlargements onto a screen or wall. Like any device, projection tools can fail. Your program should never depend completely on the device.

Some tips to consider:

▶ Practice using the device(s) before your presentation. Adjust the lights and screen so they are most effective.

▶ Focus and zoom your images before your presentation.

International participants at this talk are invited to share nature-related words in their language on a projection of a world map.

- Bring the audience's attention back to you by turning off the projector or using a black screen during transitions.
- Direct viewer attention by pointing to specific parts of the image or object that you are projecting. Avoid pointing at the screen.
- Consider how you can creatively use projection devices. They can magnify small objects or allow you to create shadow puppets.

Audio Tools

While most presentation aids are visual, audio adds another sensory dimension that can be a powerful connector. The howl of a wolf, the crackling of a fire, or the whistle of a steam train create emotionally charged images in our minds.

Many devices are available to share audio clips with your audience, including CD players, handheld digital audio players (like iPods or MP3 players), smartphones, tablet computers, laptop/desktop computers, or hand-held animal song players. You can also create your own sounds using instruments, game calls, or creatively selected household items (a rubber band could sound like a frog).

Here are some tips when using audio:
- Cue any audio clips before starting the program.
- Audio volume should be loud enough so everyone in the group can hear. Check the volume before the program. If it isn't loud enough, you will need some type of sound amplification.

Rattling deer antlers together is an authentic way of sharing sounds with your audience.

- Use sound or music for special effects that support the theme, not simply as background.
- Use only high quality sound.
- Don't try to speak over the sound. Audio works best when the audience can focus on it without distraction.
- Repeat fast or short sounds to give the audience a second opportunity to experience them.

Video Tools

Video clips can be excellent tools for demonstrating complex principles, showing real movement and behaviors, or adding authenticity (such as a historic clip).

Like audio, many devices are available to share video clips, including DVD/Blu-ray players, smartphones, tablet computers, and laptop/desktop computers. Unlike audio, your audience must be able to see as well as hear the video. Unless you have a small group, a large television or projection system will be necessary.

Some important tips for sharing video:

▶ Keep the video clips short and use them sparingly. The audience is coming to see you, not watch a movie.

▶ Use video clips only if there is no other way to illustrate your message. Videos tend to commandeer an audience's attention, stealing them away from the *real* experience at your site.

▶ Cue any video clips prior to starting the program.

▶ Use only high-quality video.

Multimedia Presentation Tools

A multimedia presentation combines several types of visual and audio components, including pictures/illustrations, animation, audio clips, video clips, and text. Many software programs are available for creating multimedia presentations—Microsoft PowerPoint, Apple Keynote, and Prezi are some of the most popular.

While a multimedia presentation can be a powerful way to interpret resources, it requires careful planning, development, and practice to be successful. See pages 137–151 for details about presenting effective illustrated talks and multimedia programs.

A portable television cart serves as a convenient tool for showing video clips.

Notes and Memorization

Avoid writing a word-for-word script of your talk. Notes often become a crutch and impede your eye contact and gestures. At most, have a simple outline on a note card. If you need a cue to get back on track, simply pause, look at your note card, and carry on. Make this act seem natural. A sample note card is illustrated below.

Instead of memorizing your talk, focus on a fresh, spontaneous delivery. Effective interpreters sound natural and conversational rather than rehearsed. Visualize your talk from start to finish. Keep the main points in mind and you will be able to share the examples that illustrate them in your own words.

Practicing your program in front of friends or family is a less threatening way to prepare and build confidence.

Practice

Practicing your talk is essential for conveying your message smoothly and professionally. Just thinking through a program won't be adequate. Try giving your talk in front of a mirror so you can watch your facial expressions and eye contact. Rehearse in front of friends, colleagues, or family members using actual visual aids so you build confidence. Video record your rehearsal and play it back to assess and modify your program.

Avoid using written notes when presenting your program. At most, a note card with your main points outlined can help you stay on track.

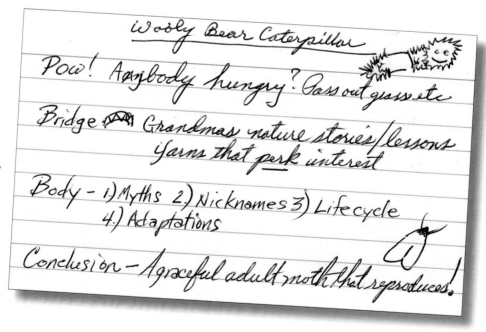

Putting it All Together

Interpretive Program Development Worksheet

To simplify the process of structuring your talk, we recommend using a Program Development Worksheet, like the example to the right. It includes space for writing your sub-themes, brainstorming creative techniques, and outlining the main parts of your program.

This is a logical extension of the Theme Planning Worksheet discussed in Chapter 3, which facilitates the development of a theme statement based on tangible resources and intangible meanings.

A completed Theme Planning Worksheet and Program Development Worksheet are included on pages 134–135 for an interpretive talk titled "The Secret Lives of the Biting Bugs." Program delivery techniques are illustrated on page 136.

 Download a blank version of this worksheet for your program development.
www.interphandbooks.org

During a program called "The Secret Lives of the Biting Bugs," an interpreter involves audience members by demonstrating how deer ticks hunt for their hosts.

Interpretive Program Development Worksheet

Presenter Name: _____

Presentation Location: _____   **Day and Time:** _____

Program Theme:

List the subthemes of your program *(2–4 "chunks" of the theme)*:

  1.

  2.

  3.

  4.

Brainstorm creative interpretive techniques you can use *(presentation style, props, involvement)*:

Outline the main parts of your program *(be as specific as possible)*:

  1. POW! *(attention-grabbing introduction)*

  2. Bridge *(transition from POW! to body: introduce self, establish credibility, incorporate theme)*

  3. Body & Transitions. (List the order of the main points. For each, provide a short description of what you'll talk about, techniques to interpret it, and transitions between the points)

  4. Conclusion *(creative and inspiring take-home message)*

Interpretive Program Theme Planning Worksheet

Presenter Name: James Biteya

Presentation Location: Mosquito Hill Nature Center **Day and Time:** June 12, 1–2 p.m.

Program Topic: The Secret Lives of the Biting Bugs

Narrow your topic through research/brainstorming and write a theme:

1. List specific resources used for research: *(primary & secondary sources)*

   Mosquito: A Natural History of Our Most Persistent and Deadly Foe (Spielman, 2001)
   Scanning electron microscope photos of biting bugs, Museum of Science, Boston, MA
   Horse and Deer Flies/Deer Ticks: Medical Entomology website, Purdue University
   Dr. Hans Driver, Entomologist, University of Minnesota, correspondence

2. List the tangible resources and intangible meanings/universal concepts of your focused topic:

Tangibles	Intangibles/Universal Concepts
Biting mouth part adaptations	Despised by humans
Life cycle of mosquitoes, flies, ticks	Romance of mating rituals
Requirement of blood for producing young	Family togetherness
Compound eyes for detecting movement	Thrill and adventure of the hunt
Antennae used for sensing sound	Empathy toward biting bugs

3. Program Theme: *(complete sentence, specific & focused, links tangibles to intangibles, tool for organization)*

   Although despised and cursed by humans, the life cycles of biting bugs such as mosquitoes, deer flies, and deer ticks are teeming with romance, adventure, and cunning adaptations in an endless quest for life-giving blood.

Describe how your program will address the Three Pillars of Interpretation:

1. How will this program meet the goals of your agency or organization?

   The mission of Mosquito Hill is to foster understanding, appreciation, and sound stewardship of the natural world. This program will reveal the lives of creatures that are often misunderstood by people.

2. What audience(s) do you expect will attend? *(ages, background, interests and expectations)*

   Primarily families and local youth groups, interested in discovering more about biting insects. They expect hands-on activities, lots of interaction, and an entertaining format.

   How will you serve diverse audiences? *(people with disabilities, minorities, older adults, families)*

   Will use a variety of techniques to engage the widest number of people and learning styles: characters, props, demonstrations, involvement activities

3. What specific site-based resource(s) will you interpret?

   Common bugs that are adapted to feeding on blood: mosquitoes, deer flies, and deer ticks.

Interpretive Program Development Worksheet

Presenter Name: James Biteya

Presentation Location: Mosquito Hill Nature Center   **Day and Time:** June 12, 1–2 p.m.

Program Theme: Although despised and cursed by humans, the life cycles of biting bugs such as mosquitoes, deer flies, and deer ticks are teeming with romance, adventure, and cunning adaptations in an endless quest for life-giving blood.

List the subthemes of your program *(2–4 "chunks" of the theme)*:

1. Mosquitoes, flies, and ticks have unique biting mouthparts adapted for penetrating skin.
2. Biting bugs have life cycles (their family) that revolve around the need for blood.
3. The mating rituals of biting bugs are diverse and perhaps even romantic.
4. Biting bugs have fine-tuned hunting strategies and adaptations for seeking their hosts.

Brainstorm creative interpretive techniques you can use *(presentation style, props, involvement)*:

Dress up in character as a mosquito, deer fly, and deer tick (antennae, compound eye glasses, wings, beak); models of different biting mouth parts; involvement activity using straws to penetrate "skin" (plastic wrap) and drink "blood" (Kool-Aid); enlarged photos of adaptations; mating ritual demonstrations

Outline the main parts of your program *(be as specific as possible)*:

1. **POW!** *(attention-grabbing introduction)*
   Ask who has heard the story of Dr. Jekyll and Mr. Hyde, and then provide a brief summary of the premise. Reveal that I am a mad scientist who has developed his own potion, and will be testing it out today for the first time.

2. **Bridge** *(transition from POW! to body: introduce self, establish credibility, incorporate theme)*
   Introduce myself and my longtime interest in insects. Describe my hatred of bugs that bite. Explain that my potion will turn me into different biting bug species, so we can understand them better, find their weaknesses, and ultimately exterminate them. <u>Transition:</u> Drink potion and transform behind a curtain.

3. **Body & Transitions.** *(List the order of the main points. For each, provide a short description of what you'll talk about, techniques to interpret it, and transitions between the points)*

   1. <u>Mosquito character</u> (sad, wimpy personality): Sad that humans hate their species so much. Explain that females have mouthparts that make it comfortable to be bitten. Blood drinking activity. Describe the mosquito life cycle. Involve audience in mosquito mating rituals. <u>Transition:</u> Change behind curtain.

   2. <u>Deer fly character</u> (high energy, jokester): Enjoys harassing humans with aerobatics. Explains that females' mouthparts are designed for speed... tearing and drinking quickly. Blood drinking activity. Describe the deer fly life cycle and "high flying" mating ritual. <u>Transition:</u> Change behind curtain.

   3. <u>Deer tick character</u> (tough, soldier): Distinguished as a superior arachnid. Explains the tick life cycle and that both males and females eat blood. Audience activity to demonstrate hunting techniques. Blood drinking activity. Describe mating ritual. <u>Transition:</u> Change back into scientist behind curtain.

4. **Conclusion** *(creative and inspiring take-home message)*
   Mad scientist returns and asks the audience what they learned from the biting bugs so he can exterminate them (provides a brief summary). Has a change of heart after understanding them better, and becomes a biting bug lover.

Sample Talk Delivery Techniques

The structure of the "Secret Lives of the Biting Bugs" talk is built from a specific theme. It features three characters—a mosquito, deer fly, and deer tick—who reveal their unique personalities, adaptations, and behaviors. The program content is organized in a similar format to facilitate the audience's ability to remember the information in "chunks" or subthemes. Diverse techniques were incorporated to encourage multisensory involvement and engage various learning styles.

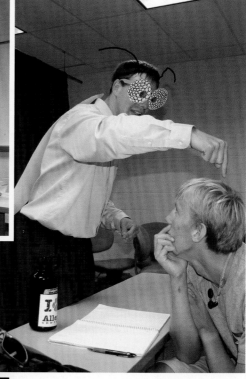

Body language is used to convey the personality of each character, like this hyperactive deer fly with a crude sense of humor.

A simple costume helps the interpreter share the essence of a character, like this depressed male mosquito with a proboscis and feathery antennae. An overhead projector is used to enlarge photos of his life cycle.

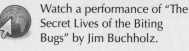

Provocative models and props, like this female deer tick pierced through plastic wrap "skin," show important characteristics and encourage involvement.

Watch a performance of "The Secret Lives of the Biting Bugs" by Jim Buchholz.

www.interphandbooks.org

Illustrated Talks/ Multimedia Presentations

Stanley Temple, a senior fellow with the Aldo Leopold Foundation, delivers an illustrated talk about using Leopold's phenological records to understand climate change.

Illustrated talks, supported by large projected images, are a staple program for frontline interpreters. They have been used effectively since the very beginning of the interpretive profession. When the Free Nature Guide Service started in Yosemite in 1921, one of the program types offered was "formal lectures, illustrated with lantern slides." Early park naturalists conducted evening illustrated talks to showcase the wonders of the parks.

Visual images dramatically connect visitors with resources or transport them to different places and times. People are naturally drawn to projected images, as is evidenced by the popularity of television, films, and smartphones.

The rapid evolution of computers, digital projectors, and software make illustrated talks and multimedia presentations easier than ever to create and share. However, the misuse of tools like PowerPoint gives these types of presentations a bad reputation.

This section introduces interpretive techniques for developing effective illustrated talks that support your theme and engage the audience.

History of Illustrated Talks

People have always been fascinated by projected images. We can imagine cave people sitting around a fire making shadow animals on the walls. The earliest "projectors," developed in the 1400s, were simple metal cylinders with shapes cut out of the sides and lit by a candle.

The invention of the "magic lantern" in the 1650s allowed an image painted on a glass plate to be focused through a lens onto a wall. Magic lanterns remained a popular form of entertainment and education for nearly 300 years. Wandering lanternists traveled the countryside putting on small shows in houses and inns. People flocked to large theaters to view the wonders of the world, scientific demonstrations, and even horror shows projected onto screens.

Magic lanterns were popular entertainment and educational tools for nearly 300 years.

When photography emerged in the mid-1800s, it was the perfect match for magic lanterns. The black-and-white photos, printed on glass plates, were often painstakingly colored by hand.

By the end of the 1800s, magic lanterns were common in homes, schools, lecture halls, parks, and other public facilities. The first interpreters used photographic lantern slides to entertain and inform large audiences about the unique natural and cultural features of their sites.

The introduction of 35-mm Kodachrome color film in 1936 revolutionized illustrated talks. Magic lantern shows were quickly replaced by sleek, "modern" slide shows. Small, transparent slides were less expensive to develop and easier to store. Projectors automatically changed slides with the push of a button. Slide shows became a mainstay of interpretation for the next 60 years. Nearly every nature center, visitor center, historic site, and park had slide projectors—and many are still in storage!

The emergence of affordable computers, digital cameras, and digital projectors in the mid-1990s ushered in a new era for illustrated talks. Software programs like Microsoft PowerPoint, Apple Keynote, and Prezi allow presenters to freely import images, sort them on screen, and add text and effects. Today, digital multimedia presentations have largely replaced slide shows.

Benefits of Illustrated Talks

Although the specific tools have changed, interpreters have presented illustrated talks for nearly 100 years. They continue to be a popular method for communicating with an audience. Why are these presentations so successful?

- **They attract and hold people's attention for long periods of time.** People are naturally drawn to storylines that include images.
- **They reveal resources in dynamic and provocative ways.** They can show elusive wildlife, dynamic landscape changes, or stories from the past.
- **They can present powerful take-home messages.** Studies show that people remember more when they both see and hear a presentation.
- **Images enhance the spoken word** and can sometimes relate the message without narration.
- **The presenter can respond to audience needs and questions.** Unlike a video or television show, an illustrated talk is a personal experience that creates opportunities for interaction.
- **They enhance the credibility and professionalism** of a presenter.

A ranger in Badlands National Park delivers an evening slide show talk, circa 1958.

Why Can PowerPoint Programs Be so Bad?

How do you feel when someone mentions the word "PowerPoint"? Does it conjure up images of long, boring lectures? Do you dread seeing endless slides filled with text that you frantically try to read? Does the thought of sitting through another dull presentation in a dark room make you cringe? You're not alone. Over the years, PowerPoint programs have suffered a bad reputation.

The reputation is often well deserved. Many presenters don't put the time and energy needed into developing an effective illustrated talk. Presentation software makes it almost too easy to add pictures, text, and effects.

PowerPoint is just a tool, like a magic lantern or a 35-mm slide projector. It's your job as an interpreter to learn the tool and use it to create

Don't lose your audience! Avoid the pitfalls of ineffective PowerPoint programs—too much text, a lack of images, and the presenter talking to the screen.

engaging and inspiring talks. The box below describes many shortcomings of PowerPoint programs that you likely have experienced.

Potential Issues with Illustrated Talks/Multimedia Presentations

▶ **Too much text.** Some believe that audiences will learn better if presenters put more words and bullet points on the screen. As participants try to read and listen, learning is actually reduced.

▶ **Using the screen as a note card.** Since it is so easy to add text, many speakers read off of the screen like it's a giant note card. This is simply an excuse for not taking the time to practice.

▶ **Poor image quality.** Have you ever heard a presenter say, "Sorry about the quality of this picture, but..."? Never use an image that you need to apologize for.

▶ **Multiple images on a slide.** Presenters tend to cram related images onto a single slide. Audiences are distracted by multiple elements and you lose the visual impact of a full-screen image.

▶ **Clip art clichés.** How many times have you seen the graphic of a detective with an oversized magnifying glass? Audiences tire of overused clip art.

▶ **Standard templates.** Presenters overuse the predefined templates that come installed with presentation software, which gets old for the audience.

▶ **Animation and transition headaches.** Presentations are often packed with the bells and whistles that come with the software. Animation must have a purpose or it quickly loses its appeal.

Creating Effective Illustrated Talks and Multimedia Programs

Illustrated talks and multimedia programs developed for interpretive audiences are *fundamentally different* than those presented in classrooms and at conferences. They must be engaging, provocative, and inspiring. They emphasize and support your thematic storyline through high-quality images, sound, and movement. They shouldn't rely on text, bullet points, tables, graphs, charts, or generic clip art.

The following guidelines form the foundation for developing an effective visual presentation that supports your interpretive talk.

Images are *the* most important component

People have always been drawn to illustrated talks because of the novelty of seeing images projected larger than life. They do not attend programs to see words or graphs. Photographs and illustrations are still at the core of any multimedia program. Here are some tips when working with images:

Images, like this historic photo of a migrant mother taken by Dorothea Lange during the Great Depression, evokes strong emotions without words.

Tell your story through carefully selected images. An interpreter at Schmeeckle Reserve, Wisconsin, presents an illustrated talk to introduce monarch tagging to citizen scientists.

1. Tell your story through pictures

The most enticing documentaries feature visuals that support the narrator's message. An interpretive illustrated talk follows this same premise—reveal the storyline of your theme through creatively selected visuals.

▶ **Illustrate every main point in your talk**. Develop your talk using the techniques in the beginning of this chapter before creating your visuals. Because projected images are your primary "props," each message you share should be visually supported.

▶ **Change slides at least every 10–15 seconds.** This keeps the audience actively engaged. Spending too much time on a single slide leads to eye fatigue and boredom.

▶ **Use images that creatively reveal the essence of your topic.** For a talk on painted turtles, no one wants to see a hundred pictures of the same turtle from different angles. Find creative ways to illustrate each point. An image of an armored tank, for example, might represent the turtle's shell.

Example: Tell your story through pictures

An effective illustrated talk uses images to support every main message. The example below shows how an interpreter might use visuals to discuss the life cycle of a monarch butterfly.

"Monarch butterflies have an amazing life cycle that revolves around milkweed plants."

"They start their lives as tiny eggs, about the size of a pinhead, laid on the underside of a milkweed leaf."

"After four days, a small caterpillar hatches and begins to devour the milkweed, the only plant they eat."

"Milkweed juice contains a poison. When a predator tries to eat a monarch, they get a mouthful of poison and spit it out again."

"The caterpillars continue to eat and grow for two weeks. Then they find a branch above the ground and shed their skin to form a chrysalis."

"Inside, an almost magical transformation takes place. In ten days, an adult butterfly hatches out to dry off its wings."

2. Use full-screen, high-quality images

Enhance the professionalism and attractiveness of your program with high-quality images.

▶ **Use a single image on each slide.** Don't combine multiple small images on a single slide. This reduces the size of each image and is distracting to the audience. Provide a single visual that they can focus on.

▶ **Maximize the image size on the slide proportionally**. You have an entire slide to work with. Showcase each image by increasing its size as much as possible. Resize images proportionally, so they maintain the same ratio. This means that there may be some extra space on the left and right with vertical images, or top and bottom with horizontal images. Don't stretch an image wider or thinner to completely fill the slide—this distorts the image. Use a black background instead.

▶ **Use a black background behind full-screen images.** You want the focus on the image itself. A black background matches the darkness of the screen and goes largely unnoticed by the audience.

▶ **Use only sharp, high-resolution images.** Digital photos need to be at least 1024 x 768 pixels for modern projection equipment. If the resolution is too low, you will see pixels and the image will look fuzzy.

▶ **Avoid poor quality images.** You should never have to apologize for the poor quality of an image—find a high quality alternative, or don't use it at all.

▶ **Crop images with messy edges.** Scanned photographs sometimes have visible borders that are ragged or uneven. Cropping makes them look clean and professional.

Maximize impact by resizing each image proportionally to fill the slide, keeping the same ratio.

The photo on this slide is proportional. Note how the black background is visible on the top and bottom.

The photo on this slide was stretched vertically to fill the slide. Note how the image is now distorted. This reduces professionalism.

Example: Use full-screen images

Consider the following two POW! introductions to a program about severe weather.

Program #1: Multiple images on a slide have low impact

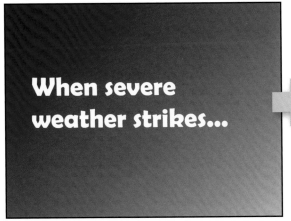 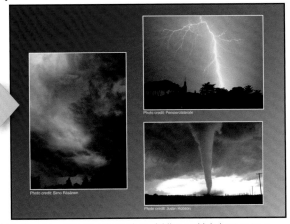

The POW! for program #1 uses two slides. The interpreter is silent and lets the slides "talk" for themselves. Adding multiple images on a single slide reduces their size and they compete for the audience's eye. The color gradient in the background creates a distraction.

Program #2: Full-screen images focus attention and have greater impact

The POW! for program #2 stretches four slides. Again, the interpreter is silent. Full-screen images are much more dramatic and vivid. They reduce competition and focus the viewer on the message. The background has been changed to black, which goes largely unnoticed.

3. Use black slides to bring the focus back to the interpreter

Just as pauses are essential to speaking, black slides are essential to the visual rhythm of an illustrated talk. They provide a momentary break in the continually changing images, snapping the audience's focus back to the presenter. This technique keeps the audience actively engaged. Black slides are ideal for transitioning to the next major point or introducing other techniques, such as storytelling or props.

4. Respect copyright

The Internet makes it effortless to find and insert an image into your talk. With a quick search, hundreds of thousands of images are available for nearly any natural or cultural history topic. As an ethical interpreter, it is your responsibility to determine who owns the copyright for any images you want to use.

The complex laws concerning copyright and fair use doctrine are beyond the scope of this book. However, to reduce the possibility of copyright infringement, use only images that:

▶ **You have taken yourself.** You automatically own the copyright on these.

▶ **Someone from your organization has taken as part of their work**. Typically, these belong to the organization.

▶ **You have received written permission from the copyright holder to use**. For example, you ask a photographer online to use their image in a program.

▶ **Are in the public domain**. These include images where copyright has expired or photos taken by employees of the U.S. government—the National Park Service, U.S. Fish and Wildlife Services, U.S. Forest Service, and other agencies have extensive photo collections online.

▶ **Are covered by Creative Commons Licenses**. These provide a way for copyright holders to allow sharing and use of images without written permission—visit Wikimedia Commons at http://commons.wikimedia.org.

Unless you use your own or your organization's images, you will typically need to credit each photo in the presentation. A small citation at the bottom of each slide with the photographer's name provides credit without distracting from the image itself.

University of Wisconsin-Stevens Point archaeologist Ray Reser uses photos from his own collection to interpret the early inhabitants of the region. The artifacts on the front table enhance the authenticity of the program.

Limit Your Use of Text

Strive to eliminate text in your interpretive illustrated talk. Words might be appropriate for classroom or conference settings where participants will be taking notes. However, recreational audiences are not coming to your program to read off the screen or take notes. They seek inspiration, enlightenment, and entertainment. Get rid of unnecessary text!

One interpreter used animated text to mimic the look of the "Law & Order" television series to interpret poisonous wildlife.

1. Text *can* be appropriate for titles, short quotes/poems, or captions

You can consider using text for some elements of an interpretive talk. For example, the title of your presentation helps to visually set expectations. A heading might work well as a transition to your next major subtheme. A short quote or poem can be better appreciated when people read it. Captions identifying something on the image eliminate the need to turn around and point. A particularly difficult or scientific word might be more understandable when displayed.

What do the following font families convey about the style and feeling of an interpretive talk on loons?

The Life of the Loon

The Life of the Loon

The Life of the Loon

The Life of the Loon

The Life of the Loon

2. If you use text, choose a font family that represents your theme

Every font has a unique character. Choose a font that matches the unique theme and style of your talk. An elegant, flowing font would fit a poetic interpretation. A comical, informal font would support a humorous presentation.

3. If you use text, make the letters large enough (larger than 24 point) to be easily seen from the back of the audience

Why use text if audience members can't see it? The size of the text will vary based on the font used, the size of the screen, and the dimensions of the room or amphitheater. In general, never use letter sizes smaller than 24 point.

4. Repeat any text out loud that you include in your slides

Despite choosing a readable font and size, some audience members will have visual impairments that challenge their ability to read off the screen. If you have a short quote, for example, say the quote out loud for your audience in addition to showing it on your slide.

Add Movement Purposefully: Transitions and Animation

Today's presentation software makes it easy to incorporate movement into an illustrated talk through transitions (movement between slides) and animation (movement on a slide). Movement adds interest and life to an otherwise static series of images.

1. Make slide transitions simple, subtle, and unified

Transitions are the movement between two slides. In a typical presentation without transitions, one slide appears instantly after another when advanced. This is a very abrupt change, which may work well for fast-moving sequences (like showing a cheetah running), but often conveys a sense of hurriedness or unpreparedness to the audience.

There are many active transitions available that include more extreme movement—3-D cubes spinning, a filmstrip advancing, shape fades, pages turning, water ripples, etc. While these add pizzazz to a program, the audience can quickly tire of the movement.

Good transitions are smooth and subtle. A "fade" transition, where one slide disappears while the next fades in, is calming and professional without being distracting. For unity, you should use the same transition style throughout the program, unless there is a good reason to change (for example, during a storytelling session or transitioning to a new subtheme).

Animation can enhance creative interpretive techniques, such as this interactive game show that reveals the characteristics of Wisconsin's mammals.

2. Use animation sparingly to reveal or add surprise

Animation is adding movement to specific elements on a slide, such as images, text, and shapes. This allows you to focus attention on a specific element (circle an important character in a historic photo), reveal different concepts (compare the difference between a viceroy and monarch butterfly), add interest or surprise (a butterfly flutters in and lands on a flower photo), and enhance creative interpretive techniques (interactive trivia game).

Like active transitions, overusing animation quickly gets tiring to the audience. Animation has more impact when used sparingly. Avoid using it just because you can—this leads to animation headaches! Animation must be thematic and have a purpose.

 Watch how an interpreter used animation to create a "Law and Order" style POW! for a program about poisonous wildlife.
www.interphandbooks.org

Audio Adds a Multisensory Component

Sound effects and music are powerful emotional connections to a topic. They add another level of sensory experience, helping engage the audience. Audio can transport people to different places and times, evoke strong memories, and create an authentic aura for your talk.

1. Check your audio and volume before presenting your program

Audio files are significantly larger than image files, which can cause issues when transferring your program to a different computer. Check that your audio is working. Copy all audio files (MP3, WAV, WMA) to your presentation folder. Practice with the actual sound system you will be using and check the volume before giving your program.

2. Move the "Sound Icon" off the slide

By default, a "sound icon" (looks like a little speaker) is added to a PowerPoint slide when you insert audio. This is distracting and gives away the surprise of sound. Move the icon off the slide and make the sound play unexpectedly as part of the animation sequence.

3. Don't talk over music or sounds

Background music is an intriguing way to create an atmosphere for your program. However, if you talk over the audio, it can be distracting to audience members who are trying to listen to both you and the music. This is especially true for those with hearing impairments. Play the music or sound, fade it out, and then begin talking again.

Hearing a wolf howl evokes powerful emotions. Move the "sound icon" off the slide so it doesn't detract or give away the surprise.

The sound of people laughing and talking around a crackling campfire can bring this static historic photo to life.

Music creates an ambience and can transport the audience to a different era. An interpretive program about the influence of Elvis Presley wouldn't be complete without hearing the songs that made him famous.

Short Video Clips Can Interpret Complex Topics

Video clips—those that show moving images with or without sound—are ideal for demonstrating complex moving topics, such as the behavior of wolves, the slow motion hovering of a hummingbird, the operation of a steam engine, or the calving of a glacier. They can also add authenticity to an illustrated talk, like archival video of John F. Kennedy's inauguration speech, a field expert describing a recent find, or actual footage of a supernova.

A video showing a hummingbird hover in slow motion enhances understanding of their complex wing movements.

1. Limit the number of video clips used and keep their length to 30 seconds or less

Interpretive audiences come to your program to hear *you*, not watch a movie. Anyone can do a quick search online and watch a video clip or a documentary. Interpretive talks are unique because they are personal. Use a video clip *only* if it is the best way to illustrate a point. Often, a prop or demonstration will work even better. Keep the video clips as short as possible—30 seconds or less.

2. Cue the video ahead of time for smooth transitions

Video sharing websites like YouTube or Vimeo are rich resources for interpreting a diversity of topics. A smooth transition between your illustrated talk and showing the video is absolutely necessary for a professional presentation. Before your program, cue the video at the correct spot. No one wants to listen to advertisements, so make sure you are past these. Check the speakers and the volume if the video has sound.

Historic footage of lumberjacks in the 1900s felling large trees adds authenticity and transports the audience to an earlier era.

3. Consider narrating the video yourself

Instead of just playing the narration that is part of a video clip, try developing an interpretive message that you can deliver while the video is playing. This gives you the benefits of video but keeps the personal nature of delivering an interpretive talk.

Delivering an Interpretive Illustrated Talk

Creating an effective sequence of visuals for your illustrated talk is only the first step. Be sure to review all of the techniques required for presenting effective talks in this chapter. Beyond the talk basics, presenting an illustrated talk requires some special techniques to be successful.

The Visuals and the Talk Should Stand Alone

In an effective illustrated program, the interpreter focuses all of their attention on the audience and presents the talk as if the images aren't there. The images serve merely as visual support for the interpreter's messages.

If something happens to go wrong with the computer or projection equipment, you can still present your program without the slides.

- **Do not verbally refer to your slides.** Avoid using statements such as "This is a picture of . . .", "As you can see . . . ", or "This shows . . ."
- **Avoid turning and pointing to show things on a slide.** This reduces your eye contact with the audience. If possible, use animation to highlight the element.
- **Do not talk to the projection screen or computer screen**. We have a tendency to stare at screens and use them as a crutch rather than make eye contact with our audience. Practice the presentation enough so you know which slides are coming up next without looking. A momentary glance every once in a while will ensure you are in the correct spot.

An interpreter at Cumberland Island National Seashore, Georgia, presents an illustrated talk about the unique wildlife of the sanctuary.

- **Do not present a travelogue.** When someone shows you pictures from their vacation, they give a travelogue, their account of the trip. Interpretive talks are based on a theme rather than a visual journey.

Don't Be Tethered to the Computer

Many illustrated talks are delivered with the presenter behind a desk staring at a computer screen, clicking with a corded mouse. As an interpreter, your primary focus is always the audience.

- **Use a cordless mouse or wireless presenter.** These handheld devices allow you to advance slides from nearly anywhere in the room. They are small and discreet. They give you freedom to move and use your hands for gesturing. Presenters often point them at the screen or computer when changing slides, which isn't necessary. Practice advancing slides subtly and naturally.

▶ **Stand in front of the audience, but avoid blocking the screen.** Like all interpretive talks, don't hide behind podiums, desks, computers, or notes. Stand in front of the audience, make eye contact, and be engaging. Movement is a bit more restricted for illustrated talks since you don't want to block the view of the screen. Be conscious of where people are sitting and the space where you can move safely.

Prepare and Practice

Have you ever witnessed a presenter struggling to get their presentation to work right while the audience watches and waits? This sends a cue that the presenter is ill prepared and unprofessional. Planning for unexpected scenarios and practicing are essential for successful delivery of illustrated talks.

▶ **Practice using the actual equipment.** When possible, practice your illustrated talk with the actual computer and projector that you will use for your final presentation. Every piece of equipment works a bit differently. The fonts may not be the same. Sound might not work. You may not be able to access the Internet.

▶ **Always have a backup copy of your presentation available.** If you have your presentation stored on a single flash drive and the drive fails, you're out of luck. It is easy to back up your program on different devices or online so you're ready for the worst.

▶ **Incorporate other interpretive techniques and involve the audience.** While projected images are the main visuals of an illustrated talk, you still need to use effective interpretive techniques to involve and engage your audience. Consider questions, activities, storytelling, demonstrations, and props. Diverse techniques serve the multiple learning styles of your audience.

An interpreter at Schmeeckle Reserve, Wisconsin, presents an illustrated talk about flying squirrels.

Checklist for Presenting Effective Illustrated Talks

- ▶ Develop your talk before creating your multimedia presentation.

- ▶ Tell your story through pictures; illustrate every main point in your program.

- ▶ Change slides every 10–15 seconds.

- ▶ The majority of slides should be full-screen images; avoid putting multiple images on a single slide.

- ▶ Use images that reveal the essence of your topic in unique and interesting ways.

- ▶ Use only high-quality, sharp images.

- ▶ Use black backgrounds so the attention is on your images.

- ▶ Incorporate blank black slides into the presentation to bring the focus back to the speaker.

- ▶ Respect image copyright; include credit lines on slides for images you have permission to use.

- ▶ Avoid using text, except for titles, short quotes/poems, or captions. When used, choose a font that reflects the character of your talk and a large enough size to be seen from the back of the room.

- ▶ Choose a unified transition style between slides that is simple and thematic.

- ▶ Use animation sparingly and with purpose.

- ▶ Sound effects and music clips add an engaging sensory component; check your audio and volume before starting the program and don't talk over them.

- ▶ Use video only if it is the best way to illustrate your message. Limit clips to 30 seconds or less, and cue them before starting your program.

- ▶ Look at the audience, not the projection or computer screen.

- ▶ Your talk should stand alone from your images; don't refer to your slides.

- ▶ Use natural movements and body language by using a cordless mouse or presentation device.

- ▶ Stand in front of the audience, but avoid blocking the screen. Don't hide behind podiums, desks, or computers.

- ▶ Practice with the actual computer and projector system that you will be using.

- ▶ Have several backup copies of your presentation.

- ▶ Incorporate other interpretive techniques to support the visual projected images; involve the audience.

 Achieve "PowerPoint Enlightenment" by experiencing the good and bad of illustrated talks with Jim Buchholz.

www.interphandbooks.org

 Listen to comedian Don McMillan present "Life After Death by PowerPoint," a humorous look at bad PowerPoints.

www.interphandbooks.org

References

Structure Your Talk

- Cowan, N. (2005). *Working memory capacity: Essays in cognitive psychology*. New York, New York: Psychology Press.
- Ham, S. H. (2013). *Interpretation: Making a difference on purpose*. Golden, CO: Fulcrum Publishing.
- Ham, S. H. (1992). *Environmental interpretation: A practical guide for people with big ideas and small budgets*. Golden, CO: North American Press.
- Laskowski, L. (1998). How to use transitions effectively. LJL Seminars. http://www.ljlseminars.com/transit.htm
- Moscardo, G. (1999). *Making visitors mindful: Principles for creating sustainable visitor experiences through effective communication*. Sagamore Publishing: Champaign, IL.
- Myers, D. G. (1986). *Psychology*. New York, NY: Worth Publishers.
- Ward, C. W. & Wilkinson, A. E. (2006). *Conducting meaningful interpretation: A field guide for success*. Golden, CO: Fulcrum Publishing.

Illustrated Talks/Multimedia Presentations

- Bryant, H. & Atwood, Jr. W. (1932). *Research and education in the National Parks*. Washington, D.C.: United States Government Printing Office.
- The Magic Lantern Society. (2007). A history of the magic lantern. Retrieved from http://www.magiclantern.org.uk/history/

Image Citations

All photos copyright of the authors unless noted below.

- Pp. 116–117: Courtesy of Aldo Leopold Foundation
- P. 118: Courtesy of Megan Espe
- P. 121: A Common Loon in Marshfield, Vermont, USA, courtesy of Ano Lobb at Flickr (CC BY 2.0)
- P. 122: Kevin Stonerock photo by Brett Roller, kevinstonerock.com
- P. 124: Seeds of Vincetoxicum rossicum in October, Toronto, bank of Humber River, Canada, courtesy of Mykola Swarnyk at Wikimedia Commons (CC BY-SA 3.0)
- P. 128: Interpreters with flip chart, courtesy of Spring Mountains National Recreation Area
- P. 137: The Laterna Magica by Paul Sandby, ca 1760
- P. 138: Evening campfire talk in the amphitheater at Cedar Pass Campground, National Park Service Historic Photograph Collection/photographer Jack E. Boucher
- P. 140: [Destitute pea pickers in California. Mother of seven children. Age thirty-two. Nipomo, California.] By Dorothea Lange, 1936. Library of Congress, Prints and Photographs Division, [LC-USF34-T01-009093-C]

- P. 141: Monarch with wings spread, courtesy of Bob Mosier
- P. 141: Blue jay eating monarch and vomiting, courtesy of Lincoln P. Brower, Sweet Briar College
- P. 141: Monarch emerging from chrysalis, courtesy of Sid Mosdell at Flickr (CC BY 2.0)
- P. 142: Deer fawn, courtesy of Bob Mosier
- P. 143: Lightning; fulmine caduto su Roma durante un temporale estivo notturno, courtesy of user Pensierolaterale at Wikimedia Commons (CC BY-SA 3.0)
- P. 143: Thunder cloud; a vertical view to a thunder cloud rising above in 2010 July, courtesy of Ximonic, Simo Räsänen at Wikimedia Commons (GNU FDL)
- P. 143: Tornado; category F5 tornado viewed from the southeast as it approached Elie, Manitoba, on Friday, June 22, 2007, courtesy of Justin Hobson at Wikimedia Commons (CC BY-SA, 3.0)
- P. 147: Wolf howling; Dakota, a grey wolf at the UK Wolf Conservation Trust. Courtesy of user Retron at Wikimedia Commons
- P. 147: Campfire at Mesa Verde National Park. National Parks Portfolio, NPS photo
- P. 147: Elvis; Graceland, Memphis, Tennessee, 68 Special exhibit at Graceland Crossing, courtesy of Thomas R. Machnitzki at Wikimedia Commons (CC BY 3.0)

Website Resources
www.interphandbooks.org

Video Clips

- **The Secret Lives of the Biting Bugs example talk:** Interpreter and author Jim Buchholz presents a character program that demonstrates the use of visual aids, props, involvement activities, and questioning techniques.

- **South Carolina Aquarium example talk:** An interpreter presents a program about the Great Ocean Tank by interacting with a scuba diver inside the tank and using props.

- **Superfly Butterflies Fashion Show example talk:** Interpreter Rachel Anderson presents a creative, engaging talk about butterfly adaptations by involving the audience in a fashion show.

- **Life After Death by PowerPoint:** Comedian Don McMillan shares the most common PowerPoint mistakes in a humorous presentation.

- **PowerPoint Enlightenment:** Discover the steps that you can take toward achieving an "enlightened" illustrated talk that connects with the interests of the audience.

Documents

- **Interpretive Program Development Worksheet:** Microsoft Word and Adobe PDF downloads.

PowerPoint Samples

- **Venomous & Poisonous:** Creative POW! to an illustrated talk based on the "Law & Order" television series. Created by Briar Bush Nature Center educator Katie McAfee.

7

Guided Interpretive Walks & Tours

The essence is to travel gracefully rather than to arrive. Enos Mills

During the late 1800s and early 1900s, Enos Mills trained nature guides in what later became Rocky Mountain National Park. The first "interpretive programs" were guided walks led by these trained naturalists. An interpretive walk or tour is more than just a "moving talk." It requires a unique approach based on the dynamic features of a site and active group involvement.

Eric Anderson, a wildlife professor at the University of Wisconsin-Stevens Point, guides a walk at the George W. Mead Wildlife Area to demonstrate the tools used by wildlife managers.

Guided Walk and Tour Basics

An interpretive guided walk or tour is defined as an interpreter addressing a mobile audience. Typically, the program has several defined stops where the presenter interprets a site resource. Guided programs can vary significantly, from leading a group on a trail to touring a historic house.

Guided walks and tours are popular with visitors. Freeman Tilden recognized that people are drawn to see authentic resources firsthand. He wrote:

> In most [interpretive sites] the visitor is exposed, if he chooses, to a kind of elective education that is superior in some respects to that of the classroom, for here he meets the Thing itself—whether it be a wonder of Nature's work, or the act or work of man.

The most successful guided tours and walks are based directly on physical site resources that visitors can experience.

Tours vs. Walks

While guided walks and tours share many of the same elements, there are core differences that affect how we can best plan and present them to our audiences.

Guided Interpretive Tours

As the name implies, a guided tour is a brief trip through a specific place often for the pur-

People are drawn to see "the Thing itself," according to Freeman Tilden. An interpreter in Costa Rica leads a guided walk through a pineapple plantation.

pose of seeing all of its parts. Historic buildings, archeological ruins, battlefields, museums, and caves are prime venues for tours. Interpreters who lead tours are often called tour guides.

A tour tends to be more regimented and planned, as the visitor *expects* to see as much of the place as possible. A tour through a historic house, for example, will typically have stops at every room. A tour through a cave will visit every major chamber and formation open to the public.

The best guided tours, like all interpretive programs, are based on strong themes. However, the themes tend to be broader in order to provide a holistic overview of the entire site.

Strict timing at each stop is often critical, especially at popular sites where multiple groups are being guided on a daily schedule. An interpreter might lead the same tour multiple times in a day. Due to this repetition, tour guides have sometimes garnered a negative reputation for presentations that sound memorized and lackluster. Good interpretive guides stay fresh and inspirational to connect with the audience on a personal level, despite the number of times they give the same program.

Guided Interpretive Walks

A guided walk can offer opportunities to be more dynamic and flexible than a tour. The purpose is to show site features that revolve around a specific theme rather than touring an entire place. Nature centers, parks, wildlife areas, and sites with broad resource appeal are typical locations for interpretive walks.

The interpreter chooses the stops that best tell a thematic story. The audience doesn't expect to see the entire place, but rather be connected to their topic of interest. For a walk about mushrooms, for example, the interpreter would plan stopping points where the audience can observe different species.

While timing is still important—interpreters should always strive to stay within the advertised length of a program—a walk is flexible and more open to variation. An interpreter might discover an unexpected mushroom and stop the group to talk about it. The group might take more time at a planned stop to address a topic of particular interest to the audience.

An interpreter at Stonefield State Historic Site leads a tour of a historic house, describing life on a Wisconsin family farm in the early 1900s.

Example: Difference Between Guided Tour and Guided Walk

Historic Site Guided Tour

A tour of a historic house would typically include stops at each room, with the guide interpreting the artifacts that can be seen and experienced. The theme needs to be broad enough to encompass the entire property, such as telling the story of the family who once lived there. The audience expects to see as much of the property as they can.

Historic Site Guided Interpretive Walk

A guided walk at a historic site could be based on any number of specific themes. One theme might focus on the early production of food. Participants could be led into an heirloom garden to see the plants growing, into a root cellar where food was stored, and into a summer kitchen where food was prepared. The stops are based on the specific theme rather than touring the entire site.

Transportation Modes

Walking is the usual way of moving an audience from one place to another, but it's by no means the only way! Alternative forms of transportation, such as a Segway®, boat, or tram, allow interpreters to cover more ground and provide increased accessibility. The novelty of the transportation often attracts people who might not otherwise join an interpretive walk, expanding our audience impact.

The box below provides a sample of unique transportation options and providers for interpretive tours.

A Segway® tour group crosses over the Mississippi River on the Stone Arch Bridge in Minneapolis, Minnesota.

A naturalist at Wyalusing State Park in Wisconsin leads an interpretive canoe paddle on the backwaters of the Mississippi River.

Guided Tours: Samples of Transportation Modes and Providers

- ▶ **Bicycle tours:** Volcano Bike Tours, Volcanoes National Park, Hawaii
- ▶ **Canoe/kayak tours:** Meewasin Interpretive Canoe Tours, South Saskatchewan River, Canada
- ▶ **Horse and carriage tours:** Historic Savannah Carriage Tours, Savannah, Georgia
- ▶ **Horseback tours:** Will Rogers Trail Rides, Will Rogers State Historic Park, California
- ▶ **Dog sled tours:** Muktuk Adventures Dog Sled Tours, Whitehorse, Canada
- ▶ **Segway® tours:** Segway® Tours of Gettysburg, Gettysburg National Battlefield, Pennsylvania

- ▶ **Tram tours:** Shark Valley Tram Tours, Everglades National Park, Florida
- ▶ **Bus tours:** Historic Red Bus Tours, Glacier National Park, Montana
- ▶ **Boat tours:** Portage Glacier Cruises, Portage Lake, Alaska
- ▶ **Snowmobile/snowcoach tours:** Yellowstone Snowcoach Tours, Yellowstone National Park, Wyoming
- ▶ **Train tours:** Southern Prairie Railway, Ogema, Canada
- ▶ **Plane/helicopter tours:** Papillon Aerial Sightseeing, Grand Canyon National Park, Arizona

Benefits and Challenges

Interpretive walks and tours have several advantages over stationary programs:

▶ Walks and tours interpret real resources on the site, creating powerful and authentic connections.

▶ They are multisensory experiences—visitors are immersed in the sounds, smells, and feelings of a site.

▶ Visitors are physically involved through walking or other movement.

▶ Unplanned "teachable moments," such as a deer strutting across the trail or discovering a nest with eggs, are memorable experiences.

▶ They provide opportunities for the interpreter to interact with the audience, allowing for spontaneity.

Walks and tours also present some distinct challenges that require advance planning:

▶ External interference, such as temperature, weather, and noise, are often challenging components.

▶ Large groups can be hard to handle—as the group gets larger, it takes longer to move from place to place and it is more difficult for all group members to see and hear the interpreter.

▶ Depending on the site, visitors with mobility impairments may not be able to participate.

▶ Group size may need to be limited to avoid negatively impacting the site.

▶ The walking or tour route needs to be well planned for reasonable length, time, and accessibility.

Tips for Giving Effective Guided Walks and Tours

▶ **Interpret the site.** Guided walks and tours are especially meaningful because they interpret actual resources that can be experienced on the site. Develop a theme based on the resources. Plan brief stops that focus attention on the site.

▶ **Be a good host.** Be cognizant of the audience's comfort level. Move at an appropriate pace. Choose sheltered areas with seating options for stops. Face yourself into the wind and sun so the audience doesn't have to. Wait until everyone arrives before speaking. Find a natural stage and speak audibly.

▶ **Be prepared.** Know your site and route well. Avoid the use of notes. Start on time and stay within the advertised length of the program.

▶ **Be flexible.** Plan for alternative experiences in case of inclement weather. Be ready for unplanned "teachable moments"—these are often the most memorable parts of programs.

▶ **Involve the audience.** Speak with audience members before the program to create a personal relationship. Use a diversity of interpretive techniques, such as questions, props, and multisensory tools, to engage the audience. Plan transitions to keep the audience involved as they move from one stop to the next.

▶ **Come full circle.** The best guided walks and tours come full circle both physically (back to the starting point) and thematically (a conclusion that wraps up the theme).

Planning Your Walk or Tour

The most meaningful interpretive walks and tours showcase site resources that the audience can directly experience.

A guided moving interpretive program requires planning to be effective. You serve as both the interpreter and the group leader. Your program showcases actual resources found at the site, which are powerful connectors to the audience.

Interpret the Site

The most effective interpretive walks and tours are based on the physical site features that audience members are experiencing. Tell the story of the site. Why is it unique? What are people seeing, feeling, hearing, and smelling? Make it a sensory experience and one that helps them understand this specific location better.

It is your job as an interpreter to know as much as possible about the features and resources of your site—plants, animals, seasonal cycles, cultural history—even if they don't relate directly to your theme. Visitors are curious about the world around them, so we need to nurture and encourage that curiosity. If a flower is blooming along the trail or an unusual artifact is spotted during a historic home tour, visitors will undoubtedly ask what it is. What a great opportunity to connect them with a resource—they're already interested!

Develop a Site-Based Theme

Like all interpretive programs, a successful guided walk or tour is built around a central theme.

Because this type of program is site-specific, it is critical that you develop your theme based on the actual resources of the site.

Avoid generic "nature walks" or interpreting a topic where the site is just a background. The theme should be directly related to the site's resources. For example, if your topic is "beavers," choose a site with ample signs of beaver activity that your audience can experience firsthand. If your topic is the "history of the Mississippi River," don't just use a site where the river serves as a backdrop. Interpret specifically what happened at the spot where the audience is standing and have photos to prove it.

Many tour destinations, such as historic sites, museums, caves, or battlefields, already have a pre-determined route without much flexibility to modify. As you develop your theme, consider the route and how you can creatively tie the various stopping locations together.

Watch several examples of interpreters leading dynamic walks and tours built around site-based themes.

www.interphandbooks.org

Structure Your Walk or Tour

The structure of a guided walk or tour shares many of the characteristics of an interpretive talk (described in Chapter 6). However, since the site is the focus and the audience is moving, there are several unique characteristics to plan for. The basic structure of a guided walk or tour has five parts:

> ### Basic Structure of Walk/Tour
>
> ▶ **POW!** Capture the group's attention with a provocative introduction.
>
> ▶ **Bridge.** Introduce yourself, establish credibility, link to the theme, set expectations.
>
> ▶ **Body.** Each stop should be planned to support the theme with site features and creative techniques.
>
> ▶ **Transitions.** Keep the audience engaged between each stop.
>
> ▶ **Inspiring Conclusion.** Bring the audience full-circle thematically and physically. Present an inspiring call to action or message.

POW! Grab Their Attention

Just as with interpretive talks, you first must capture the attention of the audience. Start with an effective **POW!** Be creative about how you reveal the topic in a novel, unexpected way. If your walk is outside, you will be competing with distractions such as noise, weather, and other activities. It often takes a louder or more exaggerated delivery to really grab the group's attention. If possible, make it a sensory experience specific to the site. For example:

▶ Sight: "Look at the pine tree towering above you. How do you think it got that black scar on its trunk?"

▶ Sound: "Listen quietly to the sounds around us for a few seconds... What did you hear?"

▶ Touch: "Put out your hand and close your eyes. I'm going to put something in your hand and I'd like you to guess what it is."

▶ Smell: "As I bring this box around, take a whiff. What does the smell remind you of?"

Interpretive walks and tours are sensory experiences. Here, audience members taste sugary sap from a maple tree.

Bridge: Set Expectations

Once you have the attention of the audience, remember to be a good host. The **Bridge** of the talk addresses what the POW! means to the visitor and helps set expectations. Within the bridge of a guided walk or tour, you should:

- ▶ Warmly welcome the audience
- ▶ Introduce yourself, affiliation, and establish credibility
- ▶ Reveal the theme
- ▶ Inform them about the distance, terrain difficulty, and length of the program
- ▶ Include rules or safety information
- ▶ Remind audience members that the program is informal and to feel free to ask questions

Washington University anthropologist John Kelly leads an interpretive tour at Cahokia Mounds State Historic Park, Illinois.

Examples of Guided Walk POW! and Bridge

Example 1

"I think we're ready to get started. Welcome to Cahokia Mounds! My name is Larry and I'll be your guide. Today we're going to climb up Monks Mound, the largest prehistoric earthwork in North America. Are you ready? Let's go!"

In this first example, the interpreter introduces himself and the site but doesn't set many expectations for the experience. The introduction lacks an attention-grabbing POW! and a bridge to a specific theme.

Example 2

"Imagine standing here 900 years ago. You hear the sounds of kids playing, dogs barking, and huts being built. You smell the smoke of thousands of cooking fires. And on top of that

mound, you witness sacred ceremonies being conducted in a wood structure that soars into the heavens. This was Cahokia.

"Hello everyone and welcome to Cahokia Mounds. My name is Larry. I've always been fascinated by Native American cultures and have devoted my life to studying them. Today we'll be exploring what everyday life was like for those who lived and worked at Cahokia. Our walk will last about an hour and does require climbing about 150 steps to the top of Monks Mound. If you have any questions along the way, just feel free to ask."

The second example starts with a sensory guided imagery POW!, establishes the interpreter's credibility, introduces a specific theme, and sets expectations for the time frame and difficulty of the hike.

Body: Plan Thematic Stops

The **Body** of your walk or tour is made up of a sequence of specific stops where you will interpret your messages. A guided walk is like a pearl necklace. The theme is the central idea (or thread) that connects all of the stops (or pearls) along the way. You must carefully prepare each pearl and its placement along the string, but the visitors should only perceive the whole necklace.

The primary theme should be divided into two to four subthemes that help organize the walk. The locations for stops should be planned based on tangible site resources that support and illustrate each subtheme. These resources will serve as the focal point for each stop. The experience will be supplemented through other creative interpretive techniques such as props, pictures, storytelling, or activities.

Tips for developing your route include:

▶ At each stop, the site resource(s) should be the focus of attention. What can visitors experience here that they can't experience elsewhere on the route?

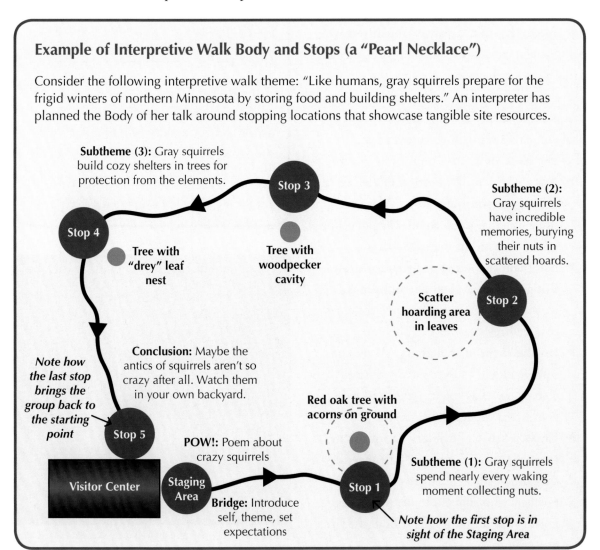

Example of Interpretive Walk Body and Stops (a "Pearl Necklace")

Consider the following interpretive walk theme: "Like humans, gray squirrels prepare for the frigid winters of northern Minnesota by storing food and building shelters." An interpreter has planned the Body of her talk around stopping locations that showcase tangible site resources.

Subtheme (3): Gray squirrels build cozy shelters in trees for protection from the elements.

Stop 3

Subtheme (2): Gray squirrels have incredible memories, burying their nuts in scattered hoards.

Stop 4

Tree with "drey" leaf nest

Tree with woodpecker cavity

Scatter hoarding area in leaves

Stop 2

Note how the last stop brings the group back to the starting point

Conclusion: Maybe the antics of squirrels aren't so crazy after all. Watch them in your own backyard.

Red oak tree with acorns on ground

Stop 5

POW!: Poem about crazy squirrels

Staging Area

Visitor Center

Stop 1

Bridge: Introduce self, theme, set expectations

Subtheme (1): Gray squirrels spend nearly every waking moment collecting nuts.

Note how the first stop is in sight of the Staging Area

- Each stop should have a clear purpose and support one or more subthemes. A subtheme may be illustrated at multiple stops.
- Stops should be brief; plan about 5 to 7 stops for a one-hour hike.
- As much as possible, stops should be evenly spaced along the entire route (not too close or too far from each other).
- Be sensitive to the interests of the group.

Transitions: Engaging the Audience between Stops

Keep the audience engaged as you move from one stop to the next. Creative **Transitions** will help the audience stay focused on your theme while allowing them to experience the surroundings on their own terms. Travel at a speed that is comfortable for your audience, which is likely much slower than you are used to.

Some ideas for creative transitions include:

- **Ask a provocative question related to the message at your next stop.** "As we continue walking, think about what an eclipse might have meant to early settlers."
- **Ask them to look at or listen for something specific in their surroundings.** "As we walk to our next stop, watch for clues that squirrels may have left behind."
- **Involve them in an activity.** "As we continue walking, collect as many different colored leaves as you can find, and we'll compare at the next stop."
- **Create a sense of mystery about the next stop.** "At our next stop, we'll be meeting a creature with serrated jaws and slicing pinchers who happens to be quite hungry. Fortunately for us, it's only about the size of a peanut."

Conclusion: Come Full Circle

The **Conclusion** of a walk or tour should bring the audience full circle, both physically and thematically. Connect it back to your POW! and theme. Like an interpretive talk, the conclusion should leave the audience with an inspirational message that provokes them to discover more.

Example Walk Conclusion

"We've returned to the shade of this 200-year-old oak where we began. This gnarled tree has seen a lot. It began like the acorn you're carrying. One acorn in a thousand might sprout a seedling and one in a million grow as majestic as this giant. When you rest under an old oak, listen to the whispering leaves and imagine the drama it has witnessed. Someday it will die, decay, and become the nurturing soil for a sprouting acorn . . . and a new story. Enjoy the rest of your visit and keep an eye out for all those creatures, real and mythical, that are sneaking around in the oak grove!"

The conclusion of a walk inspires a visitor to pause and reflect in an ancient oak savanna in Schmeeckle Reserve, Wisconsin.

Effective Walk/ Tour Presentation Techniques

Once you have outlined the structure of your walk or tour, it is time to focus on how to most effectively deliver the messages to your audience. A guided walk is fundamentally different than a stationary talk. The audience depends on you not just as a presenter but also as a leader who can guide them through a landscape and resolve any issues that arise. The following techniques will help you deliver a successful and meaningful walk or tour.

Be a Good Host

Being a good host is an important part of any interpretive presentation, especially with guided walks and tours as they typically take place outside and are subject to the elements. As a host, you need to consider the comforts and needs of your guests.

Check the Route and Prepare Alternate Experiences

Be prepared. You should be very familiar with the route you will be taking. On the day of the program, be sure to consider the following:

- ▶ Check the trail or tour route conditions. Are the paths clear, safe, and accessible?
- ▶ Are there logistical concerns that may require a detour? For instance, if a barge is coming into the lock chamber during the

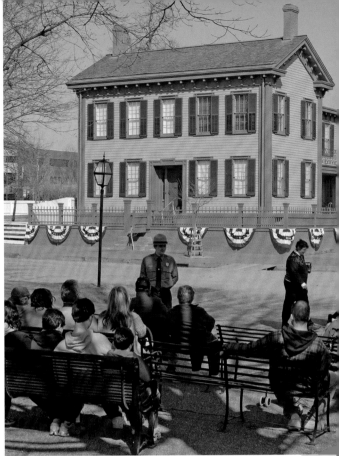

A staging area, like this shaded seating area at Lincoln Home National Historic Site in Springfield, Illinois, serves as an obvious gathering place and encourages interaction between visitors and the interpreter.

tour, or construction is occurring, what alternate route will you take?
- ▶ In case of inclement weather, be prepared with a backup plan, such as moving the program indoors or under shelter.

Set Your Staging Area

The staging area is where your group will gather before starting the program. It may be just outside a visitor center or historic home or at a trailhead where participants can easily find you. This starting point should be communicated clearly with signs, announcements, and the help of coworkers to avoid any confusion about where the program starts.

Understanding your audience's needs and abilities is an important part of being a good host. On this wildflower hike at Powers Bluff Park in Wisconsin, visitors rest on a nearby boulder.

Mingle with the Group Before the Walk

Arrive at the staging area at least 15 minutes early. Talk with your guests to gain insight into their interests and backgrounds. This facilitates an important personal dialogue with the audience and encourages interaction during the program. It can also increase your comfort level—the audience is no longer made up of strangers.

Some questions you might ask:

▶ "Where are you from?"

▶ "What are you enjoying about the park/historic site/nature center?"

▶ "Did you see any interesting wildlife during your visit?"

▶ "How did you hear about the program?"

First impressions are critical. Before uttering a word, your credibility is expressed by your appearance and behavior. Be professional in a casual manner. Remove barriers with the audience, such as sunglasses or a hat, which could prevent good eye contact with the group.

Starting the Program

You will typically begin your program at the staging area where visitors gather. This allows time for latecomers to join. Here are some tips for the beginning of your program:

▶ Start on time. Even if other guests are running late, you owe it to the participants who made the effort to arrive on time.

▶ Project your voice. This is especially important when speaking outside or with a large audience.

▶ Use a creative POW! to catch attention. See page 161 for details.

▶ Set expectations for the walk or tour in your Bridge. See page 162 for details.

▶ Plan the first stop within view of the starting point to give latecomers a chance to catch up with the group.

Keep Visitors Comfortable and Safe

Unlike stationary talks, interpretive walks and tours often require audiences to physically move through environments that have changing conditions. The interpreter is responsible for ensuring that visitors are as comfortable as possible. Some techniques include:

▶ The interpreter should face into the sun or wind so the audience is turned away from the distraction.

▶ Set a comfortable pace for walking, which is usually much slower than you're used to. This will be based on the people in your group. Audience members with mobility impairments may require a slower pace.

▶ Provide opportunities for sitting and resting where possible.

- In hot, sunny weather, choose stops that provide shade. In windy or drizzly weather, find sheltered locations.
- Carry a first aid kit, water, and a radio (or other device) to communicate in an emergency. Ideally, interpreters leading walks and tours should have first aid training.

The End of the Program

The conclusion of your program brings the walk full circle, both physically and thematically. Here are some recommendations:

- The program should conclude near the staging area to enhance wayfinding. If this is not practical, offer to guide the group back to the starting point.
- Leave the audience with an inspirational message. See page 164 for details.
- Graciously thank your audience for attending the program and encourage them to explore the site on their own.
- Following the program, be available to answer additional questions or talk to visitors about their experience.

Expect the Unexpected

Guided walks and tours are dynamic experiences unique to every audience. Be prepared for the unexpected. Those serendipitous "teachable moments" when a deer crosses the trail, a chickadee sings on a nearby branch, or a fish leaps out of the water are events that an audience may remember for the rest of their lives.

Visitors often ask questions that you didn't anticipate. Intimately knowing the site and its resources is an important foundation for being able to answer unexpected questions. If you don't know the answer, be honest. Bring along resources, like identification guides or historic documents, that can be referenced. Offer to assist the visitor in searching for the answer after the program.

The challenge of these types of events and questions is not only interpreting something "on the spot," but also finding ways to tie it back to the theme of your walk. Always keep the theme at the forefront of your mind, and creatively weave your spontaneous messages back to the main idea of your walk.

Visitors on a canoe tour in Everglades National Park, Florida, experience a chance encounter with a Roseate Spoonbill feeding.

Gadgets/Gimmicks Bag

An essential tool for interpreters leading guided walks and tours is a gimmick bag or backpack filled with interpretive aids to involve the audience. Just as with interpretive talks, it is important to show tangible examples to support the main points of your walk and increase visitor understanding.

Gadgets involve the senses and serve as tools to focus attention. Use your imagination. Gain inspiration from your local hardware store, grocery store, flea market, or from your own closet! The following are some broad ideas of what you might include in your bag.

An interpreter shows a thermometer to demonstrate how the temperatures of cold-blooded animals change. A gadgets/gimmicks bag is essential for keeping your props, pictures, and other tools organized on an interpretive walk or tour.

Props/Objects

Guided walks and tours are based on tangible site resources that people can experience with their senses. Often this means that your props and objects are naturally occurring, such as a wasp nest hanging from a tree, witch hazel blooming in October, an old farm implement rusting in the weeds, or a stone foundation of an old building.

To truly reveal your topic, however, consider creative physical objects that support your sub-themes. A simple walking stick can turn into a pointer that directs attention. A mirror focuses attention by reflecting light into a treetop cavity. M&M's in a jar represent the number of mosquitoes a bat eats in a night. See page 94 for general tips about using props.

Natural areas, historic sites, and caves often preserve sensitive artifacts and features that should not be touched. Interpreters can carry props, such as "sacrificial" artifacts or replicas, to satisfy the visitor's urge to touch.

Pictures/Illustrations

While the main experience is the site itself, visual images can support your message and showcase resources that might not otherwise be seen on the walk (for example, wildlife, geologic processes, or historic photos).

- ▶ Pictures and photographs need to be large enough for the group to see and of high quality. Affix the images to a hard backing so they are manageable in wind. Protect pictures from the elements with lamination or plastic.

- ▶ Drawings that depict something, such as cloud formations or deer adaptations, should be prepared prior to the walk to save time. Use markers with high contrast.

- ▶ Maps can be useful for orienting your audience or highlighting principles such as population densities or ranges. Be sure that the map is not too cluttered or complicated. Keep it simple.

Multisensory Tools

Guided walks and tours are often conducted in environments brimming with rich sounds, smells, and textures—birds singing, water dripping, a breeze blowing, the sweet scent of flowers. Focusing the audience's attention on their senses is a powerful way to connect them to the site.

Sensory tools in your gadgets bag can be used to enhance the experience. You might play and challenge your group to mimic the call of a Barred Owl to see if a real one responds, share the smell of fresh pine sawdust when describing the logging era, pass around a muskrat pelt to feel its warmth, or offer a taste of Arborvitae tea that cured scurvy in early explorers.

To be effective, a multisensory tool must be more interesting than distractions in the environment. For example, an audio recording must have enough volume that people can hear it above the ambient noise.

Mobile Technology Tools

Mobile technology devices, such as tablet computers and smartphones, are increasingly popular tools to share interpretive content during walks and tours. They can show photographs, images, and maps, play sound or video clips, identify plant and animal species, and engage the audience with citizen science research opportunities.

Some interpretive techniques to use mobile devices include:

► Prepare and organize the device with images, sounds, and apps prior to the program. Practice so you can quickly access the files.

► Bring the device out only when appropriate and put it away again when finished. Avoid holding onto it through the entire program.

► Ensure the volume is loud enough to be heard over the ambient noise. If not, powered speakers may be necessary.

► Avoid using the device to show images on a sunny day, as screen glare can reduce visibility.

► Don't depend on having a connection to the Internet during your walk. Save your files on the device itself.

An interpreter uses a wildflower identification app on a tablet during a walk to showcase similar flowers.

An Interpreter's Backpack

The following list, generated by interpreters Mike Freed, David Shafer, and Bill Krumbein, offers a potpourri of tools to help you interpret natural and cultural resources. Use the list as an idea generator for your own interpretive knapsack.

- ▶ Binoculars and telescope

- ▶ Hand lens, magnifying glass, or bug box magnifiers

- ▶ Waterproof notebook: for recording ideas, thoughts, and making sketches

- ▶ Field guides and local keys

- ▶ Twine of string: for web of life game, time lines, relative distances

- ▶ Small plastic bags and bottles: for bringing home small treasures

- ▶ Large plastic garbage bags or litter bags: set a good example or keep dry in a rainstorm

- ▶ Small first aid kit or survival kit: safety is the first responsibility of the group leader

- ▶ Photographs: historic photos, aerials, and other things visitors can't see on their own

- ▶ Snorkeling mask or glass-bottom bucket: for looking below the water

- ▶ Maps: topographic, geologic, vegetation, species ranges, and historic

- ▶ Flashlight: for probing trees, rock cavities, burrows, or shining for wildlife eyes at night

- ▶ Pocket mirror: for flashing some sunlight on your subject or looking into a tree cavity

- ▶ Old dental tools: for probing flowers and other delicate things

- ▶ Tape measure: comparison of the circumference of trees and measuring

- ▶ Thermometers: measure the temperature of air (cold blooded animals), soil (compost), and water (streams vs. lakes)

- ▶ White cloth and charcoal: for making rubbings of tombstones, tree bark, and signs

- ▶ Plaster of Paris and tin cans: for making casts of animal tracks or leaf prints

- ▶ Flag tape: for temporarily marking things of interest

- ▶ Spray bottle: for photographic effects and spider webs

- ▶ Small shovel or trowel: soil and plant samples

- ▶ Collection nets: for airborne or aquatic insects

- ▶ Pocket knife: for opening seeds, prying off bark, or whittling

- ▶ Specimens: liven up your program with a few dead animals, scat, and eggs

- ▶ Recordings of sounds: bird or frog calls, steam locomotives, oral histories, songs

- ▶ Coffee filter: for filtering life out of pond water

- ▶ Tossing rings (hula hoops): for plant and soil studies. Throw them in the field, let the area they encircle be your area of discovery

- ▶ Infrared detector: used at night for observing nocturnal animals.

- ▶ Magnet: test magnetic properties of rocks and sand

- ▶ Book of Native American legends and myths

- ▶ Journal and diary quotes: from explorers or settlers of the region

- ▶ Copies of old newspaper articles about events in the area

- ▶ Musical instruments: a replica of an instrument of the era can add entertainment

- ▶ Puppets: hand puppets can be easily made and fit into a backpack

- ▶ Food samples: give visitors a taste of edible plants or historic food items

- ▶ Artwork: copies of paintings, woodcuts, and etchings show historical developments

- ▶ Historic artifacts and tools: old keys, obsolete implements, railroad tickets, coins, gold pans, logging equipment

Managing Large Groups

In a stationary interpretive talk, large audiences are relatively easy to address, as long as you project your voice loud enough (or have amplification) and have a setting conducive to everyone being able to see you (like an amphitheater or stage).

A large audience attending a guided walk or tour, on the other hand, can be a major challenge for the interpreter. Moving a large group from place to place takes time. People in the back may not be able to see or hear you well. Hands-on activities, such as touching a pelt, slows down the pace of the program nearly to a halt. Maintaining the interest of a large group is a skill that comes with practice.

To be successful, you must act as the visible leader of the group. Enos Mills understood that managing people is one of the most important,

An interpreter at Lost River Cave in Kentucky stands on a stump so the audience can see and hear him more clearly.

and difficult, tasks of a guide. He wrote:

> *[The guide] has control of his party so that he may entertain, instruct, and command without their being aware that he is ruling with a hand of iron when the best results of the trip demand it.*

The box below describes techniques that you can use to manage large groups.

Techniques for Managing Large Groups

▶ **Be a visible leader for the group.** Speak clearly and confidently, and set expectations up-front. Convey instructions for the group to follow—"Let's gather around this area so everyone can see." "Please step to the side of the trail to let the hikers pass."

▶ **Wait for everyone to arrive before speaking.** This can take longer than expected with certain audiences. While you're waiting, strike up some informal conversations with nearby guests to enhance the personal connections.

▶ **Find a natural "stage" to speak from.** At your stop, try to set yourself off from the bulk of the group so they can better see and hear you. Step off the trail or path. Stand on a rock, stump, chair, or

incline. On narrow boardwalks or paths, you might even step into a stream or wetland.

▶ **Walk past the site you plan to interpret and then double back.** Lead about half of the group past your next site to be interpreted. Then step off the path and walk back to the site. The observers will form a natural arc around you.

▶ **Plan involvement activities carefully.** Hands-on activities are ideal methods to engage your audience. Involving everyone in a large group, however, can drastically slow down the pace of the program. Bring more than one object if you plan to pass something around. Involve a few participants and invite others to interact after the walk ends.

Putting it All Together

Theme Planning and Walk Development Worksheets

A Program Development Worksheet is an ideal tool for planning the structure of your guided walk or tour. A blank worksheet is available on page 133. It includes space for writing your subthemes, brainstorming creative techniques, and outlining the main parts of your program (POW!, Bridge, Body & Transitions, and Conclusion).

This program worksheet is a logical extension of the Theme Planning Worksheet discussed in Chapter 3, which facilitates the development of a theme statement based on tangible resources and intangible meanings.

A completed example Theme Planning Worksheet and Program Development Worksheet are included on pages 173–174 for an interpretive walk called "Quaking Aspen: Live Fast, Love Hard, Die Young." Program delivery techniques are illustrated on pages 175–176.

Download a blank version of this worksheet for your program development.
www.interphandbooks.org

An interpreter reveals the pioneering characteristics of quaking aspen trees as part of his "Live Fast, Love Hard, Die Young" interpretive walk.

Interpretive Program Theme Planning Worksheet

Presenter Name: Ronald Poplar

Presentation Location: Trembling Woods State Forest   **Day and Time:** October 4, 10–11 a.m.

Program Topic: Quaking Aspen: Live Fast, Love Hard, Die Young

---

Narrow your topic through research/brainstorming and write a theme:

1. List specific resources used for research: *(primary & secondary sources)*
   Trees: Their Natural History (Peter Thomas, 2014)
   Nature Detectives, "Awesome Quaking Aspen Trees," Boulder County, CO (Fall 2013)
   Aspen Tree Symbolism, www.livingartoriginals.com/tree-aspen.html
   Carrie Florez, Forester, City of Boulder, CO, interview

2. List the tangible resources and intangible meanings/universal concepts of your focused topic:

Tangibles	Intangibles/Universal Concepts
Long, flat petioles allow leaves to shake	Strength of community (aspen clones)
Most widely distributed tree in N. America	Living landscape of sound and movement
Sexual and asexual reproduction	Challenges of being a pioneer on the edge
Clone in Utah is world's largest organism	Endurance
Used to make chopsticks, matches, pulp	"Precious gold" of aspen leaves

3. Program Theme: *(complete sentence, specific & focused, links tangibles to intangibles, tool for organization)*
   Aspen trees are pioneers that thrive in the cold north because of their unique adaptations to live fast, reproduce efficiently, and resist decimation from hungry herbivores and disease.

Describe how your program will address the Three Pillars of Interpretation:

1. How will this program meet the goals of your agency or organization?
   Trembling Woods State Park wants visitors to understand its forest management plan, which includes maintaining mixed age classes of aspen stands for wildlife habitat.

2. What audience(s) do you expect will attend? *(ages, background, interests and expectations)*
   Audiences will include families from the forest campground and members of the Poplar Paper Mill Workers Union, who are hosting their annual picnic at the park.

   How will you serve diverse audiences? *(people with disabilities, minorities, older adults, families)*
   The walk will take place on a universally accessible trail to include people of all mobility abilities. Various sensory and involvement activities will be incorporated to meet the needs of different learning styles.

3. What specific site-based resource(s) will you interpret?
   1. Young and expanding clone of aspen with exposed sucker sprouts. 2. Buck rub and porcupine chewings on aspen sapling. 3. Mature stand of aspen with hollow cavities, wood borers, bark beetles, and "eyes." 4. Low-hanging leafy branches with clinging insects waiting to be shaken onto a sheet for study.

Interpretive Program Development Worksheet

Presenter Name: Ronald Poplar

Presentation Location: Trembling Woods State Forest **Day and Time:** October 4, 10–11 a.m.

Program Theme: Aspen trees are pioneers that thrive in the cold north because of their unique adaptations to live fast, reproduce efficiently, and resist decimation from hungry herbivores and disease.

List the subthemes of your program (2–4 "chunks" of the theme):

1. Aspen trees grow fast and flimsy, but their long flattened leaf petioles "spill" wind that could break the brittle trunk and flip away insects that feed on them.
2. Aspens are hardy pioneers that produce scores of offspring, such as seeds that blow far away and clones that cling to the parents and home ground.
3. Aspen's fast growing soft wood is a great source of hollow nest cavities, and the lightweight wood is perfect for the production of crates, plywood, insulating fiberboard, match sticks, excelsior, and paper pulp.
4. The photosynthetic green bark of aspen produces energy, even when the leaves are absent, and is a rich food source for browsing animals when other foods are dormant.

Brainstorm creative interpretive techniques you can use (presentation style, props, involvement):

Play Faron Young's "Live Fast, Love Hard, Die Young" song, use a mirror to look into a tree cavity, pull up lateral clone roots from ground, involve audience in shaking insects from low-hanging branches onto a sheet, bring along examples of aspen products (fiberboard, match sticks, packing material)

Outline the main parts of your program (be as specific as possible):

1. **POW!** (attention-grabbing introduction)
   Ask the audience to listen to the chattering murmur of aspen trees all around them. What are the trees telling us? They are whispering the secrets of how they live. Play the song clip, "I wanna live fast, love hard, die young, and leave a beautiful memory..."

2. **Bridge** (transition from POW! to body: introduce self, establish credibility, incorporate theme)
   Introduce self and childhood memories of swinging on aspen branches. Theme: Today we will be exploring the adaptations of aspen trees to survive in the short growing season of the north. Describe trail conditions and walk length. <u>Transition to first stop</u>: Watch the movement of aspen leaves; why do they tremble?

3. **Body & Transitions.** (List the order of the main points. For each, provide a short description of what you'll talk about, techniques to interpret it, and transitions between the points)
   <u>Stop 1</u>: Low-hanging aspen branches. Describe the flattened leaf petioles that "spill" wind and flip away insects. Shake branch to flip insects onto a sheet. <u>Transition</u>: How do aspen trees reproduce?
   <u>Stop 2</u>: Large aspen clone and "eyes." Reveal how aspens reproduce by blowing seeds and lateral roots that produce clones. Dig up lateral root to show length and sprouts. <u>Transition</u>: Watch for wildlife in trees.
   <u>Stop 3</u>: Aspen with nest cavity. Describe how soft wood is ideal for the development of nest cavities. Use mirror to look inside cavity. <u>Transition</u>: Look for markings on the bark. Why is it so smooth?
   <u>Stop 4</u>: Porcupine chewed bark and buck rub. Explain how the green bark produces energy and is a food source for animals. Have visitors touch animal markings. <u>Transition</u>: What do aspen trees do for us?
   <u>Stop 5</u>: At trailhead in grove of aspens. Reveal and show common items made out of aspen: matchsticks, packing material, crates, paper, animal bedding.

4. **Conclusion** (creative and inspiring take-home message)
   Without the hardy, thriving aspen pioneers, we couldn't experience this living landscape of movement and sound that defines our northern woodlands. Listen carefully to the whisper of our aspen trees, and you will hear them say, "Live fast, love hard, die young... and leave a beautiful memory."

Sample Interpretive Walk Delivery Techniques

The "Quaking Aspen: Live Fast, Love Hard, Die Young" interpretive walk was built from a site-based theme. The stops were selected based on actual resources the audience could experience—an aspen clone with sucker sprouts and lateral roots, low-hanging leafy branches that showcase the flat petioles, a woodpecker cavity, "eye" markings on the bark, porcupine chewings, and a white-tailed buck rub. At each stop, the interpreter used creative techniques to reveal subtheme messages that directly supported the main theme of the program.

Audience involvement is key to a successful interpretive walk. The long, flattened petioles allow aspen leaves to flutter in a breeze, flipping insects off of them. Here, one visitor shakes a branch while others hold a sheet to catch the numerous insects that fall off.

The interpreter points out the characteristic "eye" pattern of an aspen tree formed from a branch scar. Interpreting genuine resources of the site is a primary goal of guided walks and tours.

Stop 3

Stop 4

A gimmick bag can invite involvement during a guided walk. Soft aspen wood provides cavities for birds and mammals. Here, the interpreter uses a mirror to illuminate and observe the inside of a cavity, showing a different perspective.

Limber aspen saplings serve as sparring partners for white-tailed bucks to rub the velvet off their antlers. Audience members are encouraged to feel the smooth areas where the bark has been polished, providing a physical, tactile experience.

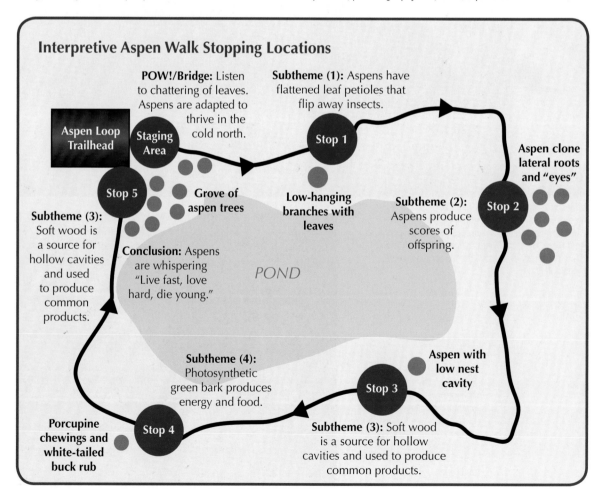

Interpretive Aspen Walk Stopping Locations

Aspen Loop Trailhead

Staging Area

POW!/Bridge: Listen to chattering of leaves. Aspens are adapted to thrive in the cold north.

Subtheme (1): Aspens have flattened leaf petioles that flip away insects.

Stop 1

Stop 5

Grove of aspen trees

Low-hanging branches with leaves

Subtheme (2): Aspens produce scores of offspring.

Stop 2

Aspen clone lateral roots and "eyes"

Subtheme (3): Soft wood is a source for hollow cavities and used to produce common products.

Conclusion: Aspens are whispering "Live fast, love hard, die young."

POND

Subtheme (4): Photosynthetic green bark produces energy and food.

Aspen with low nest cavity

Stop 3

Porcupine chewings and white-tailed buck rub

Stop 4

Subtheme (3): Soft wood is a source for hollow cavities and used to produce common products.

References

Guided Walk and Tour Basics

▶ Tilden, F. (1957). *Interpreting Our Heritage*. Chapel Hill, NC: The University of North Carolina Press.

▶ Drummond, A. (2002). *Enos Mills: Citizen of Nature*. Boulder, CO: University Press of Colorado.

Effective Walk/Tour Presentation Techniques

▶ Mills, E. (1920). *The Adventures of a Nature Guide*. Garden City, NY: Doubleday, Page & Company.

An Interpreter's Backpack

▶ Freed, M. & Shafer, D. (1982). Gimmicks and Gadgets. *The Interpreter, 13*(3).

▶ Krumbein, B. (1983). A Gimmicks and Gadgets Potpourri. *The Interpreter, 14*(4).

Image Citations

All photos copyright of the authors unless noted below.

▶ P. 158: A Segway® tour group crossing the Mississippi River on the Stone Arch Bridge in Minneapolis, Minnesota, courtesy of user Appraiser at en.wikipedia (CC BY-SA 3.0)

▶ P. 162: Cahokia Mounds Hike, courtesy of Lynn deLearie, Trailnet, at Flickr (CC BY-SA 2.0)

Website Resources
www.interphandbooks.org

Video Clips

▶ **Allegiance to Revolution interpretive tour example:** Boston National Historical Park Ranger Eric Hanson-Plass enthusiastically leads visitors on a tour of the Freedom Trail.

▶ **Burgess Shale interpretive hike example**: Yoho National Park interpreter Claudia Harding guides visitors on a full-day hike to rich fossil beds. Visitors share their experiences along the way.

▶ **Surviving a Wisconsin Winter interpretive walk example:** Interpreter Erin Cole leads a walk interpreting how different animals prepare for and survive the winter.

▶ **The Past Comes to Life interpretive walk example:** Interpreter Christine Kuhn leads a walk through a cemetery, interpreting the symbols found on headstones and telling the stories of people buried there.

▶ **Shark Valley Tram tour example:** A naturalist leads visitors on a tram tour through the northern region of Everglades National Park, pointing out numerous wildlife species along the way. At one stop, she walks out into the wetland to demonstrate its sponge-like properties.

Documents

▶ **Interpretive Program Development Worksheet:** Microsoft Word and Adobe PDF downloads.

8

Spontaneous Interpretive Encounters

It usually takes me more than three weeks to prepare a good impromptu speech. Mark Twain

Serendipitous experiences can be especially memorable and meaningful adventures for people. Most visitors to recreational sites never attend a scheduled interpretive program. Impromptu, informal interactions with visitors in the field or at an information desk allow us to share important messages with the greatest diversity of visitors. While the interactions themselves are spontaneous, thorough preparation is necessary to make the most out of these invaluable experiences.

A U.S. Army Corps of Engineers park ranger assists a young participant at an eagle watching event along the Mississippi River in Rock Island, Illinois.

Spontaneous Interpretation Basics

Spontaneous interpretation, also known as informal or roving interpretation, is a natural extension of our conversation with visitors. While an informal contact with visitors may seem impromptu, it requires advance planning, preparation, and practice to be successful.

Only about 20 percent of visitors attend formal interpretive presentations, such as evening campfire programs or guided walks, according to National Park Service research. Informal interpretive encounters are opportunities to reach a more diverse audience with our messages.

Benefits and Challenges

Informal personal contacts allow an interpreter to better assess the visitors' needs and facilitate their experience with the resource. Specifically, spontaneous interpretation allows you to:

▶ Interpret dynamic seasonal events and special occurrences that can be experienced in the moment.

▶ Provide a personal connection to the site and resources.

▶ Promote public relations (visitors appreciate one-on-one contact with staff).

▶ Assist in resource protection (convey rules where the effect is obvious and immediate).

▶ Advertise programs and events.

▶ Gain a better understanding of the visitors coming to your site.

A roving interpreter at Corkscrew Swamp Audubon Sanctuary in Florida interacts with a group on the boardwalk.

Interpreters in spontaneous settings also face unique challenges:

▶ Since visitors and serendipitous events determine the topic, you must have an in-depth understanding of site resources.

▶ Your time with individuals is typically very brief, requiring a great deal of interpretive effort for messages to be effective.

▶ You need to find ways to engage visitors on the site itself, which requires extra attention to open body language, friendly demeanor, and provocative conversation starters.

Roving Interpretation

Nature is dynamic. Few interpretive programs can fully interpret the ever-changing environment at our sites. Roving interpretation is a technique where interpreters move around the site to informally engage with visitors face-to-face as they are experiencing the resources. An interpreter roaming the site can alert visitors to exciting but fleeting events.

Effective roving interpreters must comprehend the site and its stories in-depth. They station themselves at locations where visitors naturally gather and have questions, such as a popular wildlife viewing area, the enclosure of a dynamic animal in a zoo, or an intriguing artifact at a historic site.

Search for stories to share with your visitors. Prepare interpretive responses for common questions and dynamic events that you can present when needed.

Discovery Carts/Stations

Discovery carts are portable interpretive stations that cover a variety of natural and cultural history topics. They typically hold objects and artifacts that can be touched and they offer hands-on activities. They are popular in museums, zoos, aquariums, and other high-traffic sites.

A discovery station is a staging area for spontaneous interpretation. An interpreter guides visitors to understand the theme through activities, concise messages, and answering questions. Since they are mobile, stations can be moved to natural gathering points to maximize use.

Preparing for Spontaneous Encounters

While it seems contradictory to plan for something spontaneous, preparation is essential for making the most out of informal encounters with visitors. U.S. Forest Service interpretive specialist Nikki Hinds offers several recommendations for preparing to interact with visitors in a spontaneous setting:

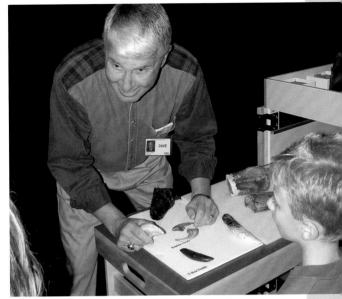

A docent at the Milwaukee Public Museum in Wisconsin uses a discovery cart to demonstrate differences between herbivorous and carnivorous dinosaurs.

▶ **Know your resource and keep learning.** If a visitor asks a question that you don't know, research the answer so you are prepared the next time.

▶ **Write roving outlines.** Consider the most popular topics visitors ask about. Write down a theme statement and one or two supporting ideas for each. You may not use the exact theme statement while roving, but if you haven't considered its importance you will likely miss an interpretive opportunity.

▶ **Develop short interpretive programs to answer common questions.** Consider the most commonly asked questions at your site. Then plan and practice a 2–3 minute interpretive "impromptu" program that you can share to answer those questions.

▶ **Learn from your peers.** Shadow more experienced interpreters while roving to see how they answer questions and engage visitors.

- **Practice effective body language.** Your body language must show that you are available and interested in interacting with visitors and answering their questions.
- **Learn to listen.** Spontaneous encounters are conversations where the visitor chooses the topic and its direction. Listening is essential to meet the visitors' needs.

Enhancing Visitor Experience

Informal one-on-one contacts with interpreters are especially meaningful and memorable for visitors. Every contact is unique and special, providing an opportunity to connect with visitors on a personal level.

For example, in 2013, the **South Carolina Aquarium** in Charleston decided to invest more in their spontaneous programs to make greater interpretive impacts outside of daily scheduled programs. The staff identified "speed bumps," strategic places where interpreters would engage with visitors as they were mov-

Visitors interact with roving interpreters at "speed bumps" at the South Carolina Aquarium in Charleston.

ing from one exhibit to the next. Interpreters were stationed with discovery carts, props, and live animals, and some visitors were even given surprise behind-the-scenes tours.

The results of these increased efforts on visitor experience were dramatic. According to an annual survey conducted by the Morey Group, overall visitor satisfaction rose by 15% for those who interacted with an interpreter compared to those who had not. Their perception of the educational experience rose by 14%, and their rating of admission value increased by 15%.

Tips for Roving and Discovery Station Interpretation

- **Position yourself in prime locations** where people naturally congregate, such as scenic overlooks, wildlife viewing areas, or near intriguing artifacts.

- **Know the site resources and its stories.** Have references handy and anticipate questions that will be asked.

- **Use "pick-up lines" to catch attention and start a conversation.** Be provocative. One interpreter asked visitors, "Did you see the Naked Ladies down there?" referring to the common name of wildflowers growing. Another asked, "Want to hold my poop?" for a discovery station about scat.

- **Props, artifacts, live animals, or tools** are excellent ways to attract attention. A portable discovery cart with thematic objects serves as a focal point and can be moved from place to place. These attention-grabbers help begin conversations.

- **Keep in mind that not all visitors may want to be approached,** so know how to read the signs and be courteous.

- **Be sure not to linger too long and overstay your welcome.** Learn to read body language and avoid keeping visitors for longer than they desire.

Case Study: Mendenhall Glacier, Tongass National Forest, Alaska

Mendenhall Glacier Visitor Center is in Juneau, Alaska, in the Tongass National Forest. The easy accessibility for cruise ship passengers and spectacular views attract about half a million visitors between May and September. Tour buses pick up visitors from cruise ships and allow about an hour on site. With such a limited amount of time, most visitors choose not to participate in a formal interpretive program. The staff relies on spontaneous interpretive encounters to reach the largest number of visitors. Some techniques to reach this fast-moving audience are illustrated below:

Use props! Mendenhall interpreters are often seen walking around with a photo, a few porcupine quills, or a small container of glacial silt. Not only do visitors enjoy the props, but it also opens the door for conversation. Here, the interpreter compares a chunk of glacial ice formed under great pressure to an ordinary ice cube. It is a sensory experience—the compressed ice snaps, crackles, and pops as it melts.

Use "ambush interpretation!" Mendenhall has several common locations where people tend to gather. Interpreters use portable microphone units and provide "impromptu" short programs at these popular sites. Typically, a visitor asks a question and the interpreter answers the question in the form of a 2–3 minute mini-program to the whole audience. Visitors don't know a program is coming but tend to appreciate the "ambush."

Case Study: Corkscrew Swamp Audubon Sanctuary, Florida

At Corkscrew Swamp Sanctuary in Florida, trained volunteer naturalists roam the boardwalks through an ancient forest of giant bald cypress trees teeming with wildlife. They often station themselves at places where visitors naturally gather or next to a spotting scope focused on hidden wildlife: a cottonmouth snake next to a cypress log or a pair of wood storks at their nest. Wildlife sightings in the swamp are dynamic. An interpreter's conversation with visitors revolves around what can be seen that day and questions the visitors ask.

A naturalist at Corkscrew Swamp helps visitors discover wildlife in the cypress swamp.

Learning stations are set up at key locations on the boardwalk to attract visitors and interpret important concepts.

Case Study: Colonial Michilimackinac, Michigan

Costumed interpreters at Colonial Michilimackinac at the Straits of Mackinac in Michigan interact informally with visitors at stations throughout the fort. At each station, interpreters are given specific interpretive themes and messages to communicate, as well as appropriate activities to demonstrate, such as blacksmithing, uniform repair, hearth cooking, and gardening. This promotes informal conservations that communicate larger historic and cultural themes.

Young "recruits" learn if they are fit for duty at this army recruiting station with the post commandant.

Inside a merchant's house, an interpreter demonstrates hearth cooking and the process of preparing a meal.

Information Desks/Stations

An interpreter offers both information and inspiration at the front desk of the Denali Visitor Center in Denali National Park, Alaska.

Park information desks are really "service stations." Imagine pulling off a highway looking for a service station. You want directions, refreshments, and gasoline. You spot an off-brand station, but it is difficult to find the driveway. An inattentive employee, feet propped next to the cash register, thumbs through a magazine. A search reveals a dirty bathroom door that is "locked for your protection." You approach the disheveled employee and ask, "What highway do I take to get to Indianola?" Without looking up, he nods to a faded map on the wall. You leave, vowing never to return.

Make your information station say, "You are welcome here. We are here to serve you." It should be visible, well lit, and accessible. Clean bathrooms and maps and brochures should be clearly available. Soft background music or nature sounds offer reassurance in indoor settings. The sight of a uniformed interpreter promises answers to questions.

Information duty is an opportunity to give visitors more than they came for. You offer visitors a gift of knowledge that will enrich their experience at the site. A well spent moment may live on as a positive memory of the visit.

Since only one in five visitors actually attend scheduled interpretive programs, take advantage of these face-to-face occurrences. You may be the only representative from your agency or organization that the visitor has contact with, and you want them to leave with a new sense of discovery or realization about your site.

Visitors often ask the same questions at an information desk. Where are the restrooms? What can I do here? Where are the best trails? Where can I see wildlife? While answering these questions becomes repetitive, approach each encounter with a fresh and enthusiastic attitude.

While visitors are typically seeking tangible facts at an information desk, these encounters are ideal for connecting them with the special meanings of your site. Reveal natural and cultural stories that relate to their interests. Interpret unique features that visitors might not otherwise discover. Advertise other interpretive opportunities, such as programs, exhibits, or visitor centers.

Tips for Interpreting at Information Stations

▶ **Look professional and approachable.** Your grooming and clothing should reflect your agency, not your personal fashion tastes. Be clean, well groomed, and understated.

▶ **Be friendly.** Respond immediately to an arriving visitor. Make eye contact, smile, and exhibit warm body language.

▶ **Focus attention on your guest.** Avoid personal conversations with other employees. Avoid answering the phone while talking to a guest, unless absolutely necessary.

▶ **Anticipate questions and be prepared with answers.** What are the "can't miss" features at your site if someone is staying an hour, a half day, a full day, or multiple days? Where are the best trails?

Where can I see wildlife? When does the campfire program begin? You can't anticipate all questions, but experience will tell you which ones you must know. Answer questions completely and concisely.

▶ **Interpret the rules.** Research shows that person-to-person contacts are more effective at communicating rules than signs and publications. Important rules should be explained and justified to visitors.

▶ **Reveal the meanings of your site.** Quickly share concise interpretive messages with visitors that reveal the special stories of the site and encourage further discovery.

Information stations, like this desk at the Grand Canyon Visitor Center, Arizona, should be brightly lit, accessible, and operated by knowledgable, friendly, and uniformed interpreters.

References

Spontaneous Interpretation Basics

▶ Knudson, D. M., Cable, T. T., & Beck, L. (2003). *Interpretation of cultural and natural resources.* State College, PA: Venture Publishing, Inc.

▶ Ward, C. W. & Wilkinson, A. E. (2006). *Conducting meaningful interpretation: A field guide for success.* Golden, CO: Fulcrum Publishing.

▶ Hinds, N. (2014, December 11). Personal communication.

Enhancing Visitor Experience

▶ Thill, B. (2014, December 11). South Carolina Aquarium. Personal communication.

Case Study: Mendenhall Glacier

▶ Hinds, N. (2014, December 11). Personal communication.

Case Study: Corkscrew Swamp

▶ Diaz, N. (2014, December 17). Personal communication.

Case Study: Colonial Michilimackinac

▶ Wilson, C. (2014, December 29). Personal communication.

Image Citations

All photos copyright of the authors unless noted below.

▶ Pp. 178–179: Courtesy of U.S. Army Corps of Engineers, Rock Island District

▶ P. 180: Courtesy of Corkscrew Swamp Audubon Sanctuary

▶ P. 182: Courtesy of Brian Thill, South Carolina Aquarium

▶ P. 183: Courtesy of Nikki Hinds, Mendenhall Glacier, Tongass National Forest

▶ P. 184: Corkscrew Swamp naturalist pointing; courtesy of Rod Wiley

▶ P. 184: Corkscrew Swamp learning station; courtesy of Corkscrew Swamp Audubon Sanctuary

▶ P. 184: Colonial Michilimackinac; photos courtesy of Craig Wilson, Colonial Michilimackinac State Park

Website Resources
www.interphandbooks.org

Video Clips

▶ **Fur trader interpretation:** A first-person character interpreter presents a spontaneous program at the Colonial Michilimackinac fur trading post.

▶ **Touch tank interpretation:** Master of Science student Shelby Boyer spontaneously interacts with visitors at touch tanks during an open house at Moss Landing Marine Laboratories.

▶ **Discovery cart interpretation:** Educator Christopher Newell demonstrates the use of "The Bison: American Icon" discovery cart at The Pequot Museum.

9

Interpretation for Children

> *He who would learn to fly one day must first learn to stand and walk and run and climb and dance; one cannot fly into flying.*
> Friedrich Nietzsche

Children comprise a large proportion of our visitors. Whether they arrive with a school, youth organization, or their family, they can contribute the enthusiasm and wonder necessary for a successful program. Special people, places, and experiences from our childhood shape our lives as adults. Lifelong commitments and interests are instilled through childhood experiences. Interpretation for children can be a vital force for shaping the future.

An interpreter at Schmeeckle Reserve, Wisconsin, guides children in an macroinvertebrate collecting activity.

Child Development for Interpreters

Children of different ages experience the world in different ways.

Freeman Tilden recognized that children's perceptions and abilities differ from that of adults. His sixth principle states:

> *Interpretation addressed to children, (say up to the age of twelve) should not be a dilution of the presentation to adults, but should follow a fundamentally different approach.*

Modern research into child development shows that Tilden's principle doesn't go far enough. Interpreters must recognize that children of *different ages* have different perceptions and abilities. Interpreters need to understand child development if they are to provide age-appropriate interpretation.

Developmental Principles

In the 1920s, psychologist Jean Piaget observed and cataloged the intellectual development of his children. Over his lifetime, he expanded on these early observations through experiments with other children—he would pose simple problems to them and, through interviews, analyze how they solved them. His well-known theories of intellectual development resulted from this work.

In recent decades, countless researchers have confirmed and expanded on these early theories. Lawrence Kohlberg examined how moral reasoning evolves. Robert Selman looked at how we assume social roles. Developmental psychologists and their colleagues have given us several principles of development:

- Child development (physical, cognitive, moral, social) is marked by times of noticeable change interspersed with times of stability.
- Child development is sequential—every child passes through a series of distinct stages. Each stage builds on the preceding one.
- Movement from one stage to another is fairly rapid, with most children changing stages at the same time.
- For a variety of reasons (experiential, physiological, sociological), development can be arrested at a lower stage.
- Teaching and interpretation must be designed for specific stages of development.

 Watch children demonstrate the different developmental stages defined by Piaget.
www.interphandbooks.org

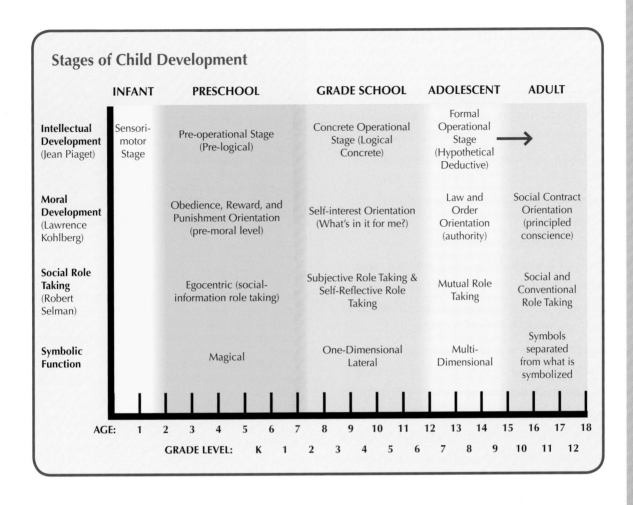

Stages of Child Development

	INFANT	PRESCHOOL	GRADE SCHOOL	ADOLESCENT	ADULT
Intellectual Development (Jean Piaget)	Sensori-motor Stage	Pre-operational Stage (Pre-logical)	Concrete Operational Stage (Logical Concrete)	Formal Operational Stage (Hypothetical Deductive) →	
Moral Development (Lawrence Kohlberg)		Obedience, Reward, and Punishment Orientation (pre-moral level)	Self-interest Orientation (What's in it for me?)	Law and Order Orientation (authority)	Social Contract Orientation (principled conscience)
Social Role Taking (Robert Selman)		Egocentric (social-information role taking)	Subjective Role Taking & Self-Reflective Role Taking	Mutual Role Taking	Social and Conventional Role Taking
Symbolic Function		Magical	One-Dimensional Lateral	Multi-Dimensional	Symbols separated from what is symbolized

AGE:	1	2	3	4	5	6	7	8	9	10	11	12	13	14	15	16	17	18
GRADE LEVEL:			K	1	2	3	4	5	6	7	8	9	10	11	12			

Interpreting for Infants *(Ages 0–2)*

An increasing number of interpretive sites are developing programs that serve parents with infants. According to Piaget, babies and infants are at the **sensorimotor developmental stage** in which they experience the world through movement and senses.

Interpretive programs developed for infants should focus on simple sensory experiences and exposure to the environment. For instance, the Irvine Nature Center in Maryland offers nature discovery walks for infants and parents that provide "slow sensory exploration" including "tactile experiences with fur, moss, feathers, leaves, and flower petals."

Sensory experiences that involve both the infant and parent are the most effective interpretive programs for this early age.

Interpreting for Preschoolers
(Ages 2–6)

Toddlers and preschool-age children are in the **pre-operational stage**, in which magical thinking predominates and motor skills are acquired. Children in this age group are egocentric (assume the world revolves around them) and animistic (give inanimate objects human-like qualities).

Preschool children are innocent and eager. To understand this developmental stage, remember these are the years of Santa Claus, a jolly old elf who flies through the air pulled by eight tiny reindeer, slipping down all the world's chimneys to leave gifts. At about age seven, children suddenly see the illogic of this idea.

Older siblings take advantage of preschool-age brothers and sisters. When offered one coin at the candy store and given a choice of a dime or a nickel, preschoolers will take the nickel, not realizing that value is not related to size.

Although they like to be with other children, they tend to play independently. They are self-oriented. All interpreters have experienced a room full of little hands going up, not to ask a question but to announce something like, "My uncle has a pet bird." Preschool children see everything in the world as alive. The sun goes to sleep like they do. Puppets are real beings.

Preschool Programs

Interpreters are increasingly being asked to provide programs for preschool children. The absence of extended families, the pursuit of careers by both parents, and the increase of single-parent families have created demand for many organizations. Parks, nature centers, zoos,

The most effective preschool programs focus on play and discovery, like finding bugs at The Ridges Sanctuary, Wisconsin.

and museums now offer preschool programs that shape attitudes and values at this important early age.

Preschool programs should focus on play, fantasy, and the senses. Group learning, if done at all, is usually limited to groups small enough to provide individual attention. However, puppet shows, story time, and other programs that engage fantasy can hold the attention of larger groups for a surprisingly long time.

The Schlitz Audubon Nature Center in Milwaukee, Wisconsin supports a popular Nature Preschool. Its mission is "to provide a high-quality early childhood environment that meets preschoolers' developmental needs while inspiring them to love nature." The curriculum integrates discovery-based learning and a hands-on approach to education.

> ### Interpretive Strategies for Preschoolers
>
> ▶ Games and play
> ▶ Puppets and characters
> ▶ Songs
> ▶ Stories (told or read)
> ▶ Sensory exploration

Interpreting for Grade-Schoolers
(Ages 7–12, Grades 1–6)

Grade-school children enter the **concrete operational stage**—they begin to think logically, but only about things that can be physically seen or experienced.

Early in this stage, children develop the ability to classify objects into categories and to order objects in a series. Conceptually, the child is ready to make order out of a complex world. Time relationships become more understandable. Dinosaurs, fanciful reptiles from the past, fascinate them. Classifying to understand the similarities and differences between groups of animals, rocks, plants, or people is of key interest.

Later in this stage, more complex concepts can be understood. A human or an animal can be seen as a member of an interacting community. Comprehending various points of view, however, is still difficult. Children in this stage are unable to manipulate complex sets of variables in their mind. For example, the complex economic, ecological, and social aspects of rainforest depletion are beyond them.

Grade-school children can reflect on their own behavior and understand right from wrong. Simple behaviors, like recycling to "save the earth," are seized upon. Although they may not know the full complexity of sustainability and other green initiatives, they will badger parents to turn off lights because their teacher told them it was "important to save energy." Subscribing to group norms is important.

Grade-School Programs

The critical ingredient for interpreting to grade-schoolers is involvement in concrete experienc-

An interpreter at the Sanibel-Captiva Conservation Foundation, Florida, demonstrates food webs with grade-schoolers.

es. Physical movement and humor is important. In a large-group program, participation can be facilitated through question-and-answer sessions.

At Fort McHenry National Historic Site, Maryland, interpreters involve children by "recruiting" them into the army. They must have good teeth to rip the paper cartridge off the musket rounds. "Recruits" are dressed in period uniform and everyone learns how various items were used.

> ## Interpretive Strategies for Grade-Schoolers
>
> ▶ Activities and games to teach concepts
> ▶ Exploration and discovery
> ▶ Sharing and empathizing
> ▶ Stories, puppets, skits, and characters
> ▶ Questioning strategies
> ▶ Devices that can be manipulated
> ▶ Physical and sensory involvement
> ▶ Metaphors

Interpreting for Adolescents
(Ages 13–15, Grades 6–9)

Adolescents move into the **formal operational stage**, where they develop abstract reasoning and logical thought processes. They can think in terms of the present, past, and future. They can also consider multiple views at one time.

Adolescents are approaching the full capabilities of adults. They can manipulate ideas even when the subject is not physically present. They can, for example, begin to weigh the pros and cons of opening up the Arctic National Wildlife Refuge to oil drilling. They can rationally defend a conclusion about the issue and apply it in a broad social context. They can think about an issue in terms of past or future, not just the present. They can contemplate the moral aspects of an issue in abstract and rational ways. They can assume the perspective of others, like Inuit fishermen, oil company executives, or wildlife biologists. Role-playing is rewarding to them.

Because of physical transformations during this stage, adolescents are boisterous and noisy, awkward and self-conscious. They fear looking weird or different. Odd behavior or appearance subjects them to the quick judgment of others. Peer acceptance is a prime consideration when choosing whether to participate in an interpretive program.

Programs for Adolescents

Young people at this age enjoy expressing opinions and assuming adult roles. Rather than reading or telling a story to them, have them read or tell it. Instead of giving a characterization, have them develop and present one.

Middle school students conduct hands-on research and discovery activities at the Sanibel-Captiva Conservation Foundation, Florida.

Simulations and games that explore complex issues or processes allow them to take other viewpoints and discover new ideas. Simulating a congressional hearing on whether to open up the Arctic Refuge to drilling allows them to consider this complex issue from a variety of perspectives.

Exploration and discovery is another involving strategy. A stream exploration, for example, could examine the health of a stream and provide useful input to natural resource management. A supervised archeological dig is an excellent way to explore a past culture.

> ### Interpretive Strategies for Adolescents
>
> ▶ Role playing in complex situations
> ▶ Assuming adult roles
> ▶ Games to explore complex issues
> ▶ Discussion and debate
> ▶ Exploration and discovery
> ▶ Simulation
> ▶ Self-directed learning
> ▶ Involvement in activities or projects

Programs for Different Ages

The Central Wisconsin Environmental Station in Amherst Junction, Wisconsin, is an outdoor teaching and learning center that offers programs for different age groups. Each program incorporates age-appropriate techniques to enhance learning and experiences.

Preschoolers independently use their senses to explore a garden.

Grade-schoolers share a salamander they discovered under a log.

Adolescents apply their existing knowledge and practice new skills to start a fire as part of a Winter Ecology course.

Working with Schools and Youth Groups

An interpreter at J.N. "Ding" Darling National Wildlife Refuge, Florida, leads a school program.

> *The parks are America's greatest classroom, telling our stories and conserving the best natural spaces the nation has to offer.*
> Parks as Classrooms, National Park Service

Most interpreters wear two hats—presenting interpretive programs to "non-captive" leisure visitors and giving educational programs to "captive" school and youth groups. The interpreter's knowledge and skill sets are very different for each audience. In addition to Tilden's principles and Meaning-Centered Interpretation, the interpreter as an educator has to know about curriculum standards, lesson plans, and merit badges. Most importantly, they must know how to collaborate with teachers and youth leaders.

Tips for Working with Educational Groups

Work closely with teachers and group leaders.

▶ Involve teachers and leaders in planning their field trip to your site, which gives them ownership of the program.

▶ Programs must fit school or state curriculum standards if teachers are to justify a field trip to your site. Work with teachers to develop standards-based programs.

▶ Post detailed information on your website about your school or youth programs. Include downloadable videos and other materials that can be used in the classroom as preparation for their visit to your site.

▶ Promote your program at teacher and youth organization meetings. Use direct mailings to alert teachers and youth leaders about your services and programs.

Prepare the students for their visit.

▶ School children and youth groups have a need to explore and become comfortable in new settings. Viewing an orientation video before the visit will help children arrive ready to learn. The orientation should include a tour of the site and an introduction to the "big ideas" of the program and activities they might participate in.

Provide an involving program.

▶ Organize the students into groups of five to ten, if possible. You may need volunteers to assist in leading the programs.

- ▶ Physical and verbal involvement of the children is essential.
- ▶ Use strategies appropriate to various grade levels and developmental stages.
- ▶ Use the resources and stories of the site.

Follow up the school/group visit.

- ▶ Help teachers or leaders find ways to use the experience for follow-up learning.
- ▶ Seek feedback from teachers/leaders and students. Use their suggestions to improve your program.

Curriculum-Based Services

Curriculum-based services assist teachers and youth leaders in meeting their educational objectives through resources offered at parks, zoos, nature centers, museums, and historic sites. The most effective services are developed by on-site interpreters and educators in conjunction with teachers.

Curriculum-based interpretive programs match interpretive goals and themes with the learning objectives of educational groups. They incorporate all of the elements of effective interpretation but differ from regular recreation-based programs in that they:

A teacher uses *A Lasting Impression* Traveling Trunk from the James A. Michener Art Museum, Pennsylvania, in her classroom.

- ▶ Address a group's specific educational objectives.
- ▶ Include planned pre-visit activities and follow-up activities to provide a sequence of learning opportunities.
- ▶ Have an audience that is known prior to the program and can be planned for (ages, backgrounds, learning styles).

Other learning-based resources are also available for teachers to provide experiences without the aid of an on-site interpreter. Some of these are listed in the box below.

Curriculum-Based Services Examples

- ▶ Pre-visit preparation activities
- ▶ Post-visit activities
- ▶ Traveling resource trunks: site or collection-based objects for a comprehensive teaching unit
- ▶ Site teacher guides/lesson plans: for teaching without an interpreter

- ▶ Teacher workshops and in-service professional development opportunities
- ▶ Educator activity guides, such as Project WILD, Aquatic WILD, Growing Up WILD, Project Learning Tree, Project WET, WOW!: Wonders of Wetlands

Behavior Management

School and youth group field trips give students engaging firsthand experiences with your site. However, an open, novel setting outside the classroom can lead to behavior issues. With a few tricks up your sleeve, you can head off most of these problems.

Ask for assistance from teachers, group leaders, or chaperones who are likely more familiar with the dynamics of the group and the children's personalities. Incorporate a variety of creative techniques to keep children involved and active—music, demonstrations, questions, puppets, and stories are well received. Above all, set expectations for appropriate behavior early and be consistent in how you respond and deal with situations.

An interpreter leads a group of Cub Scouts at the Ridgefield National Wildlife Refuge in Washington. Setting expectations with youth groups is important in maintaining positive behavior.

Tips for Maintaining Appropriate Behavior

- ▶ Set specific behavioral boundaries and expectations early in the program.

- ▶ Solicit teacher, parent, or chaperone assistance in managing problem children.

- ▶ Be consistent in handling problems; do not make unenforceable threats.

- ▶ Model appropriate behavior (e.g., pick up litter).

- ▶ Keep an upbeat attitude. Don't yell! Yelling confirms that you have lost control.

- ▶ Have activities that focus the students' attention. For example, give them a list of things to find along the trail.

- ▶ Give problem children something to do (e.g., take responsibility for your props).

- ▶ Consider injecting humor. One naturalist called out inappropriate behavior by saying, "If you keep doing that, I'll unscrew your belly button 'til your legs fall off."

- ▶ Establish a signal to get the students' attention. For example, stop the program, raise your hand, and wait until every student has raised theirs. Then continue with the program.

- ▶ Offer field trips in the morning when students are more alert, focused, and cooperative.

Interpreting with Puppets

Puppets introduce ecological principles as part of the curriculum-based EcoHelpers program in the Santa Monica Mountains National Recreation Area, California.

Puppets are an invitation to enter a fantasy world where anything is possible. Trees can talk, spirits can materialize, and wild animals can be safely petted. Puppet interpretive programs are especially appropriate for preschoolers and grade-schoolers who learn through fantasy and play. However, even adults welcome the chance to see their world in new and involving ways.

Use a puppet to deliver your message in an entertaining and engaging way. Puppets command center stage. They can interact with audience members, present controversial issues in humorous and nonthreatening ways, and personalize interpretive resources.

Puppets are also inexpensive to create and are easily stored. Carpet foam, memory foam, cloth, papier-mâché, socks, gloves, pipe cleaners, felt, paper tubes, Styrofoam balls, and other common household items can be crafted into simple and engaging characters.

 Watch an animal puppet show presented by naturalists at the Lowry Nature Center in Minnesota.

www.interphandbooks.org

Tips for Using Hand Puppets

- ► Move the puppet's mouth in sync with what is being said.

- ► Open and close the mouth with each syllable (practice in the mirror).

- ► Move the lower jaw while keeping the puppet's head level.

- ► Develop a story and stay in character. Don't spoil the impression that the puppet is alive.

- ► Puppets should make eye contact with the audience. Sweep eyes across the audience.

- ► Let the puppets carry the program. Don't lecture with a puppet on your hand.

- ► Develop a distinct personality and voice for each puppet character. The more unlike you the puppet sounds and acts, the more successful the illusion.

- ► Keep the program short and active. Five to ten minutes on stage is usually adequate for any character.

- ► Look at your puppet when it is talking. You must believe in the "realness" of your characters.

Mixed-Age Audiences

Interpretive programs usually include families with children. Your challenge as an interpreter is to develop a program that engages the whole age spectrum from children to older adults.

Children eagerly volunteer for activities, answer questions, and explore the world around them. When kids are involved, so too are the parents and other adults. A child's perspective often reveals patterns or ideas that adults might not otherwise consider and provides a humorous touch to the program.

Layering your messages is an important part of reaching the audience's full age spectrum. Start with simple, concrete concepts and engaging techniques that children can comprehend. Then build from these concepts into more ab-

A family at The Ridges Sanctuary in Wisconsin participates in a geocaching program. Interpreting to audiences of mixed ages requires layering of techniques and messages to meet the diverse needs of different age groups.

stract processes and meanings that adolescents and adults can appreciate.

Interpretation is a social activity in addition to being educational, inspirational, and entertaining. If families are present, incorporate small-group activities and discussions that encourage interaction among family members.

Tips for Serving Mixed-Age Audiences

▶ Plan for a mix of techniques and messages that can facilitate meanings for both children and adults.

▶ Choose techniques that engage children at every development stage. Parents and other adults will appreciate the messages if children are involved.

▶ Layer your messages by starting with simple, concrete concepts for children, and building to more abstract, complex concepts for adults.

▶ Carefully plan how age-specific messages will be revealed during the program. For example, when children are engaged in an activity, this is an ideal time to interpret more complex messages for adults.

▶ Creative techniques are ideal for engaging all audiences: demonstrations, questioning strategies, character interpretation, sensory involvement, physical participation, humor, storytelling, etc.

References

Child Development for Interpreters

- Schlitz Audubon Nature Center: Nature Preschool. (2014, November 3). Retrieved from http://www.sanc.org/education/nature-preschool
- Tilden, F. (1957). *Interpreting Our Heritage*. Chapel Hill, NC: The University of North Carolina Press.

How Children Learn

- National Park Service. (2010). *Park Ranger Interpreter: Module 370: Developing Curriculum-based Programs and Services.* Interpretive Development Program. Retrieved from http://idp.eppley.org/IDP/sites/default/files/DevCurrBased-370.pdf

Working with School and Youth Groups

- National Park Service. (2010). *Park Ranger Interpreter: Module 370: Developing Curriculum-based Programs and Services.* Interpretive Development Program. Retrieved from http://idp.eppley.org/IDP/sites/default/files/DevCurrBased-370.pdf

Image Citations

All photos copyright of the authors unless noted below.

- P. 190: Courtesy of Brandon R. Bowey, Washington Island Art and Nature Center
- P. 192: Courtesy of Marc Demoly
- P. 193–194: Courtesy of Sanibel-Captiva Conservation Foundation, Florida
- P. 195: Courtesy of Central Wisconsin Environmental Station
- P. 196: J.N. Ding Darling National Wildlife Refuge, Florida
- P. 197: Jarrettown Elementary School, Upper Dublin School District, PA; courtesy of the Education Department, James A. Michener Art Museum, http://www.MichenerArtMuseum.org
- P. 198: Friends of the Ridgefield National Wildlife Refuge, Washington, U.S. Fish & Wildlife Service
- P. 200: Courtesy of The Ridges Sanctuary, Wisconsin

Website Resources
www.interphandbooks.org

Video Clips

- **Examples of Jean Piaget's child development stages**: Children demonstrate key characteristics of the sensorimotor, pre-operational, concrete operational, and formal operational stages.

- **Puppet program example:** Naturalists at the Lowry Nature Center in Minnesota present monthly animal puppet shows that interpret ecological concepts.

10
Gathering Feedback

Anyone who has never made a mistake has never tried anything new. Albert Einstein

Hearing the word "evaluation" often conjures up uneasy feelings and visceral reactions. We associate the word with school exams, increased pressure to perform, and negative criticism. However, in the field of interpretation, evaluation is simply a way of acquiring feedback about your programs and techniques, which is essential for improvement. Feedback is gathered both informally by observing audience behavior and reactions, and formally through self-reflection, visitor input, and mentor observations.

Interpreters at Schmeeckle Reserve, Wisconsin, discuss the successes and challenges of a recently presented program.

Evaluation Basics

Obtaining feedback from mentors is a valuable method for improving the effectiveness of your interpretive programming.

By their very nature, interpretive programs are a subjective experience. Visitors attend programs with different expectations, needs, and past experiences, and therefore each person responds differently. This variation makes gathering generalized feedback about a program a challenge for managers and interpreters. However, assessment is essential for improving our interpretive outreach, enhancing the visitor's experience, and justifying the importance of interpretive programming.

Benefits of Evaluation

Evaluation techniques benefit not only the interpreter but also the organization and visitors to the site. Interpreters need to understand and examine what is being done, how it is being done, and what results from it. Evaluation should be considered as part of planning for interpretation, not an afterthought.

Why Evaluate Programs?

- ▶ To improve effectiveness as an interpreter
- ▶ To justify the resource cost (i.e., personnel, money, time)
- ▶ To know how well a program works or what it communicates to visitors
- ▶ To determine if the program can be improved
- ▶ To better understand your visitors and what they value

Tools of Evaluation

Interpreters and managers use many tools to obtain and share feedback. These can be divided into two categories: those that assess an interpreter (communication skills, techniques, principles) and those that assess a program (visitor satisfaction, learning, provocation). This chapter focuses on tools for assessing an interpreter. See the References on page 215 for resources to develop program assessment tools.

Tools to assess an interpreter:

- ▶ **Observing audience visual cues**
- ▶ **Structured self-evaluation**
- ▶ **Mentor evaluation**

Tools to assess a program (visitor feedback):

- ▶ **Comment cards:** Short questionnaires to gain general visitor feedback on a program.
- ▶ **Questionnaires:** Written surveys to assess knowledge, attitudes, and behavior changes as a result of the program.
- ▶ **Interviews:** Asking selected visitors brief questions about their experience and recording their responses.
- ▶ **Focus groups:** Interview, conducted by a trained moderator, among a small group of respondents.

Linking the Stages

For evaluation to be effective, it should be intertwined as an entire interpretive process that includes planning, developing, delivering, and evaluating programs. The evaluation itself occurs in multiple stages.

Since interpretive programs are presented to recreational audiences, their expectations and needs are vital to planning a successful evaluation process.

> ### Stages of Evaluation
>
> ▶ **Preparing for the program.** Identify organization's mission, understand target audience, and create program goals and objectives.
>
> ▶ **During the program.** Obtain informal feedback from the audience through visual cues and mentor observation.
>
> ▶ **After the program.** Assess the success of the program through self-evaluation, mentor evaluation, and structured visitor feedback.

Preparing for the Program

Before developing a program, interpreters create program goals and objectives based on the organization's mission and visitors' expectations. After a presentation, program evaluation targets these goals and objectives.

Agency/Organization Mission

Managers are increasingly asked to justify and quantify the effectiveness of interpretive programming. You should ensure that your program objectives help achieve the broad mission and goals of your organization or agency. See page 50 for information about knowing your organization's mission and goals.

Visitor Expectations

Interpretive programs are presented to recreational audiences. A successful evaluation process must take into account visitors' needs and expectations. Program goals and objectives should be crafted around these expectations. Satisfied visitors are the best way to promote interpretation and prove its value. See pages 51–53 for information about knowing your audience.

Develop Program Goals and Objectives

Program Goals

Goals are broad, general statements of what you intend to accomplish by presenting your program. These are drawn from your theme, your organization's management goals, and your visitors' expectations. How will the audience be impacted in terms of knowledge, understanding, or philosophy?

> **Example:** The goal of my program is to convey a sense of urgency in protecting threatened habitats, leading to participation in volunteer land management events.

Program Objectives

Objectives describe specific expected outcomes of an interpretive program that help achieve the goal. Interpretation strives to connect with people on different levels. In 1956, Benjamin Bloom led a committee of colleges to identify three major domains of educational activities, now known as Bloom's Taxonomy. Consider all three realms when developing interpretive programs and media:

▶ **Cognitive/Intellectual Objectives:** Describe what people will learn from the interpretive experience. Interpretation is an educational opportunity. But because it is just part of a visitor's recreational experience, people won't learn every small fact we provide. Focus on the theme/subthemes and reinforce them throughout.

> **Example:** After experiencing the "Return of the Timber Wolf" presentation, visitors will be able to compare and contrast differing views of animal rights groups, deer hunters, and farmers.

▶ **Affective/Emotional Objectives:** Describe what people will feel during the interpretive experience. This addresses interests, attitudes, opinions, appreciations, values, and emotions. These objectives are obviously more difficult to measure. The goal of interpretation is to guide visitors in discovering meanings in a site or resource, and an emotional connection is powerful.

> **Example:** During the fall harvest program, the scent of baked apple pie will engage visitors with a sense of nostalgia for family, warmth, and happy times.

▶ **Behavioral Objectives:** Describe how interpretive programs can influence people's behavior. What actions will visitors take following an interpretive program?

> **Example:** After experiencing a talk about freshwater jellyfish, audience members will discover more about jellyfish using outside resources.

Interpretive program evaluation examines how well the specific objectives were met, which is a measure of achieving the broader goals. Based on the results, the interpreter determines what aspects need to be adjusted or changed in future programs. See page 210 for examples of how to measure different objectives.

> ## Example of Developing Program Goals and Objectives
>
> **Program theme:** "Colony collapse disorder, where worker bees mysteriously disappear from a honey bee colony, threatens many of our common foods that depend on bees for pollination."
>
> **Goal:** To create awareness about the causes of colony collapse disorder.
>
> ▶ **Intellectual objective:** Audience members will learn that one-third of the food in our diets is directly linked to honey bee pollination.
>
> ▶ **Emotional objective:** Audience members will be alarmed by the statistics surrounding honey bee decline and concerned about their future.
>
> ▶ **Behavioral objective:** Audience members will be motivated to support organizations that are studying the causes of colony collapse disorder.

During the Program

When delivering a program, there are several ways to gain feedback. These include the instant feedback you receive from your audience and observations from colleagues or supervisors.

Feedback from Audience

As you present, observe the audience members' body language, participation, and auditory cues. Pay attention to reactions such as:

- **Interest and attentiveness:** Sitting upright, leaning slightly forward, eye contact, enthusiastic participation, asking questions
- **Understanding and approval:** Smiling, nodding, expressions like "hmmm"
- **Resistance or disapproval:** Arms folded, legs crossed, leaning back, shifting body position to the side
- **Confusion:** Confused facial expressions, head tilted, furrowed brows, no response to questions
- **Boredom:** Fidgeting with belongings, looking at a clock, whispering to neighbors, checking a phone, eyes glazed over

Feedback from Mentor

If a mentor is conducting an evaluation, they will often analyze the following aspects during your program. The interpreter will receive oral and/or written feedback after the program.

- Knowledge of the resource
- Display of passion, excitement, enthusiasm for the resource
- Ability to relate the topic to visitors' experience and knowledge
- Use of humor, human interactions, and provocation

Watching a recording of your program is an insightful self-evaluation tool.

- Ability to target different learning styles
- Skill at creating opportunities for social interaction
- Use of creative techniques
- Nonverbal communication (vocal quality, eye contact, appearance, and movement)
- Credibility, professionalism, and confidence

After the Program

After your program is complete, you have a valuable opportunity to gather feedback from multiple perspectives that will benefit your interpretive efforts, your organization, and the visitors attending your program.

Self-Evaluation

You're often your own worst critic! After a program, presenters typically focus on aspects that didn't go according to plan—forgetting to mention a fact, having trouble finding a prop, or no one answering a question. While audience members usually don't notice these nuances, it is still valuable self-reflection that leads to more effective programming.

A good self-evaluation is a journey of awareness. Begin the evaluation as soon as possible after your program while it is still fresh in your mind. You want to capture those specific emotions and insights early before they fade into a vague memory. Write down the techniques and messages that you thought worked well. Then describe those that didn't work as well.

An effective self-evaluation tool is to record your program and watch it several times to reflect on your delivery.

The first time, watch and listen to the video for an overall evaluation of the program. It takes at least one viewing to get used to seeing and hearing yourself. Watch for:

▶ Overall effect
▶ Audience response
▶ Anything that particularly stands out, both positive and negative

The second time, turn off the screen and listen only to the audio to focus on content. Ask yourself:

▶ Did you get the audience's attention at the start? Was the POW! relevant to the topic?
▶ Did you introduce yourself during the Bridge? Did you establish your credibility and introduce your theme?
▶ Did the transitions maintain flow to create obvious organization between subthemes?
▶ Did you illustrate each point with examples, stories, metaphors, props, demonstrations, activities, or visual aids?
▶ Did you ramble or stick to the theme?
▶ During the program, did you connect with both the head (logic) and heart (emotion)?
▶ Did you end powerfully? Did you connect back to your theme? Did your ending

provide a feeling of closure? Did you have an inspirational call to action?

The third time, just listen again but focus on the voice. Ask yourself:

▶ Did you vary your vocal pace, pitch, and volume in a way that supported your message and kept it engaging?
▶ How was your volume and projection?
▶ How was your use of language? Did you use any jargon or slang? Did you have good enunciation? Did you use any filler words like *um*, *so*, *okay*, *like*, or *you guys*?
▶ Did you use pauses after important points, ask questions, or use humor?

The fourth time, leave the audio on but focus on the visual. Ask yourself:

▶ How was your eye contact? Did you look down at notes, at the screen, or at your props too much?
▶ Did your facial expressions, body language (stance, movement), and gestures reinforce or distract from the message? Did they look natural?
▶ Were your attire and grooming appropriate?
▶ Did you move purposefully, or was there noticeable pacing, rocking, hand-wringing, etc.?
▶ Were your visual aids easy to see and integrated smoothly?

After evaluating your video or writing a self-reflection, you should always answer a final question: If you had the opportunity to deliver this program again next week, what are the top 1–3 changes that you would make?

Mentor Evaluation

Gathering feedback from a mentor—a supervisor, colleague, or outside expert—is invaluable to your development as an interpreter. Hearing another person's perspective broadens our view of interpretive programming and offers a creative boost borne from social interaction.

Veteran interpreter Bill Lewis conducted numerous interpretive critiques over the years with the National Park Service. He suggested that:

> *Critiquing is a process by which interpreters are helped to present the highest possible quality programs to the public. It is a continual process which incrementally moves interpreters from one level of excellence to a higher one.*

Mentors should choose quiet, comfortable spaces to share feedback with interpreters.

An oral critique is typically brief with a few main points addressed. The evaluator shares both positive feedback and constructive criticism. The oral session is often followed with a written critique that covers more detail and provides a permanent record.

DOs and DON'Ts for the Evaluator

DO:
- Choose a quiet, private, comfortable location for the critique.
- Speak in a sincere, supportive, non-threatening tone.
- Focus on a specific behavior, not on personality (e.g., "I noticed the visitors seemed to be straining to hear what was being said," instead of, "Your audience couldn't hear you; you need to speak up.")
- Start with praise before you offer constructive criticism. It is less threatening.
- Remember that you are giving feedback to fix a problem, make a positive change, and to help someone do better.

DON'T:
- Show up unexpectedly.
- Let your emotions run free.
- Follow "you" with a negative word like won't, can't, or don't.
- String together many criticisms at once. It is overwhelming. Prioritize your comments and deal with each separately.
- Give criticism to prove you are right or demonstrate your authority.

DOs and DON'Ts for the Presenter

DO:
- Welcome the chance to hear feedback.
- Maintain eye contact and open body language. This shows you want to hear the feedback so that you can improve.
- Summarize the criticism to make sure you understand it.
- Focus on solutions and how to address specific criticism. Ask yourself: What steps can I take to correct this problem?
- Feel good about the positive things being said and incorporate them into future programs.

DON'T:
- Instantly defend yourself or blame someone else. Stay calm and wait until it's your turn to respond.
- Confuse criticism with an attack on your personality or total job performance.
- Make a quick decision whether to accept or reject the criticism.
- Ignore the criticism and forget about it. Ask yourself: Have I heard similar criticism before? Am I perceived as less effective or less professional because of this criticism?

Structured Visitor Feedback

Visitors are the primary reason we present interpretive programs. To truly gauge whether a program was successful, we need to ask our audience. Tools for gathering structured feedback from visitors range from simple comment cards to in-depth interviews.

Regardless of the tool used, asking visitors to share feedback is often an extra burden during their leisure time. The visitor evaluation program must be carefully planned to be appropriate and respectful of the visitor's valuable time.

Gathering general information

Gathering general information about a program can be done quickly and unobtrusively. Observations, such as the number of visitors attending a program, indicate the comparative popularity of a topic. Comment cards are a common way of gauging the audience's satisfaction—what did they like or not like about the program?

Measuring program objectives

Gathering more in-depth information, such as whether your objectives were achieved, requires a more structured evaluation tool and more time and effort from the visitor. Questionnaires, interviews, and focus groups can be designed with questions that target the achievement of these objectives.

Some objectives are easier than others to measure. To test a cognitive objective, you can simply ask what a visitor learned. An emotional objective often requires some type of scale—for example, "On a scale of 1 to 10, to what extent did the program arouse your curiosity?"

A researcher at Lost River Cave in Kentucky interviews visitors about their experience after attending an interpretive program.

A behavioral objective is the most challenging to measure, as it requires the audience to do something in response to a program. To test short-term behaviors, such as picking up a brochure or walking a nature trail, observation can be used. Measuring long-term behaviors, like recycling more often or buying organic food, would require a major commitment to follow-up with visitors, which usually isn't practical. Measuring the *intent* to do a behavior—"How likely is it that you will buy organic food?"—is less reliable but provides a gauge for testing the potential success of the objective.

When structuring a tool to gain feedback from an audience, be sure that you first determine what you really wish to know. Don't burden your respondents with more questions than you actually need to ask. Your visitor will appreciate your respect for their time and may even give greater thought and effort to their responses.

See the References on page 215 for resources that describe how to develop different measurement tools for assessing your programs.

Interpretive Program Evaluation Form

The following two-page form is a tool that can be used to evaluate yourself or other interpreters who deliver programs. Despite the wide range of interpretive techniques and styles, there are foundational elements that lead to successful communication. This form focuses on evaluating these important criteria.

The form has four main categories divided into specific elements for analysis:

1. **Interpretive Principles:** Based on Freeman Tilden's core interpretive principles, these make up the foundation of any effective interpretation.
2. **Organization:** How a program is organized is important for the audience to follow the main ideas: theme, introduction, body, conclusion, and transitions.
3. **Interpretive Techniques:** Oral communication techniques demonstrate the quality of a presenter in front of an audience.

Elements include voice, body language, eye contact, innovative techniques, and questioning.

4. **Effort:** This category represents the time spent preparing and practicing for the presentation, and how credible the interpreter appeared to be.

For each element, the form offers a Likert-type scale of "Excellent" to "Poor," which provides quick feedback about the perceived quality. This allows the presenter to see which categories they are excelling at and which could be improved in the future. Each category also has space for comments from the evaluator.

> Download a blank version of this form to use for your own program evaluation.
>
> **www.interphandbooks.org**

A written evaluation form serves as a permanent record of feedback that can be used to enhance your interpretive programming skills.

Interpretive Program Evaluation Form

Presenter's Name: _____   Date: _____

Evaluator: _____   Program Topic: _____

Evaluators: Please provide written <u>constructive feedback</u> for each of the following four categories. Include examples of particularly effective techniques you observed and ways that the presentation could be changed to make it more effective. The items listed should be considered a source of ideas for your comments.

Interpretive Principles:

	Excellent	Good	Acceptable	Fair	Poor
Related to something within the experience of the audience					
Revealed the essence of the subject rather than simply providing information					
Developed a whole; helped audience discover meaning by linking tangibles and intangibles					
Provoked (stimulate, inspire) rather than simply instructed					

Comments:

Organization:

	Excellent	Good	Acceptable	Fair	Poor
The talk had a stimulating introduction (POW and Bridge)					
There was a well-defined theme					
The body of the talk contained clearly defined sub-themes (a manageable number)					
The conclusion left the audience with an inspirational message					
The talk contained a good flow (transitions)					

Comments:

Interpretive Techniques:

	Excellent	Good	Acceptable	Fair	Poor
Demonstrated a variety of innovative techniques (props, involvement such as demonstrations, hands-on activities)					
Used effective voice inflection and articulation					
Made the talk enjoyable and rewarding					
Avoided distracting mannerisms					
Stood in front of the audience and faced them					
Made eye contact with the audience					
Employed a variety of questioning techniques					

Comments:

Effort:

	Excellent	Good	Acceptable	Fair	Poor
The speaker displayed enthusiasm and care in preparing this talk.					
The presentation was an appropriate length (based on the advertised time)					
It was obvious the presenter had researched the subject					
It was obvious the interpreter had practiced the presentation					
The interpreter demonstrated credibility (dressed appropriately, indicated expertise, word choice).					

Comments:

Example Evaluation Form Comments

Below are comments from an actual evaluation form filled out by a mentor for a student interpreter who presented a talk on honeybees. Notice how the feedback starts out by highlighting strengths prior to moving into constructive feedback for improvement.

Interpretive Principles:

Excellent work relating the lives of honeybees to humans... references to mating, "creating" new parents, running the household, etc. You incorporated many fun techniques to reveal the essence. I didn't see many intangibles, those emotions and ideas that we feel about bees and/or honey. Rather than just providing tangible information, weave intangible meanings throughout your program to connect with your audience on an emotional level.

Organization:

The POW! worked well to reveal your topic in a creative way... I really liked the use of sound! Repeating this idea in the conclusion brought your talk full circle. The theme statement is still quite broad... lots of interesting facts about honey bees, but difficult to find the common thread. If the ONE BIG IDEA is bee communication, then make this central to every subtheme. Clearly specify your theme so the audience understands the direction of the talk.

Interpretive Techniques:

An excellent variety of techniques to reveal your topic... audience involvement using props to show different bee types, dramatic photos, specialized stingers, demonstration of waggle dance. A fun and rewarding program! Great enthusiasm and variation of tone in your voice. Be sure to avoid referencing your note cards too much... this distracts from eye contact and creates unnatural pauses in the flow. Also, avoid standing behind the desk where your note cards were located, as this creates a barrier with the audience. Good use of questioning to involve the audience.

Effort:

You have a wonderful, enthusiastic voice that spreads through the audience and makes the program fun. The timing was perfect and the research revealed fascinating aspects of honey bees. More practice will eliminate the need for note cards and help the program flow more smoothly. You introduced yourself, but be sure to establish credibility by explaining why you chose "honeybees" for your topic.

References

Evaluation Basics

▶ Ward, C. W. & Wilkinson, A. E. (2006). *Conducting meaningful interpretation: A field guide for success.* Golden, CO: Fulcrum Publishing.

Linking the Stages

▶ Atkinson, C. (2001). It's as easy as DIY. *Interpret Scotland, 4,* 4.

▶ Diamond, J. (1999). *Practical evaluation guide: Tools for museums & other informal educational settings.* Walnut Creek CA: AltaMira Press.

▶ Lewis, W. (1994). *Reaching for excellence: The process of interpretive critiquing* (video and workbook). The Interpretive Publication and Resource Center.

▶ Windingland, D. (2012, April 18). How to self-evaluate your speech. *Virtual Speech Coach Blog.* Retrieved from http://www.virtualspeechcoach.com/2012/04/18/how-to-self-evaluate-your-speech/

Image Citations

All photos copyright of the authors.

Resources to Design Interpretive Program Assessment Tools

▶ Diamond, J. (1999). *Practical evaluation guide: Tools for museums & other informal educational settings.* Walnut Creek CA: AltaMira Press.

▶ Ham, S. & Weiler, B. (2005). *Interpretation evaluation tool kit.* CRC for Sustainable Tourism. Retrieved from http://www.crctourism.com.au/wms/upload/resources/bookshop/InterpEvalToolkit_Sep07.pdf

▶ Ward, C. W. & Wilkinson, A. E. (2006). *Conducting meaningful interpretation: A field guide for success.* Golden, CO: Fulcrum Publishing.

Website Resources
www.interphandbooks.org

Video Clips

▶ **Mentor evaluation of an interpretive walk:** Interpretive trainer Bill Lewis provides mentor feedback to an interpreter (training video produced by the National Park Service).

▶ **Group evaluation of an interpretive talk:** Interpretation students at the University of Wisconsin-Stevens Point share feedback with a classmate who presented a public talk on wild rice.

Documents

▶ **Interpretive Program Evaluation Form:** Microsoft Word and Adobe PDF downloads.

About the Authors

From left to right: Ron Zimmerman, Jim Buchholz, Brenda Lackey, and Michael Gross *(photo by Doug Moore)*

Ron Zimmerman is the Director of Schmeeckle Reserve, a natural area on the UW-Stevens Point campus, where he helped develop the interpretation program in the College of Natural Resources. He is a founding member of the Interpreter's Handbook Series and the Schmeeckle Reserve Interpreters consultant team. Ron's formative years were spent in the grasslands of Nebraska.

Jim Buchholz is Assistant Director of Schmeeckle Reserve and an instructor of interpretation at UW-Stevens Point. He is a member of the Schmeeckle Reserve Interpreters consultant team and specializes in media design. Jim's enthusiasm for natural history grew from his childhood explorations of Wisconsin state parks.

Brenda K. Lackey is Associate Professor of Interpretation at UW-Stevens Point. She serves as an associate editor of the Journal of Interpretation Research and as a National Association of Interpretation board member. She worked as an interpretive park ranger for eight years with the U.S. Army Corps of Engineers on the upper Mississippi River.

Michael Gross is Professor Emeritus in the College of Natural Resources at UW-Stevens Point, where he cofounded the interpretation academic program. He initiated the Interpreter's Handbook Series and serves on the Schmeeckle Reserve Interpreters consultant team. Mike's passion for nature grew from his childhood on an Iowa farm.

Interpreter's Handbook Series

The Interpreter's Handbook Series is a collection of guidebooks developed for students and practitioners of heritage interpretation. Each book is designed to provide comprehensive, easy-to-use visual tools for conducting effective interpretive communication.

Books in Print

The Interpreter's Guidebook: Techniques for Programs and Presentations—Fourth Edition (2015). Jim Buchholz, Brenda Lackey, Michael Gross, and Ron Zimmerman

Interpretive Centers: The History, Design and Development of Nature and Visitor Centers (2002). Michael Gross and Ron Zimmerman.

Signs, Trails, and Wayside Exhibits: Connecting People and Places—Third Edition (2006). Michael Gross, Ron Zimmerman, and Jim Buchholz.

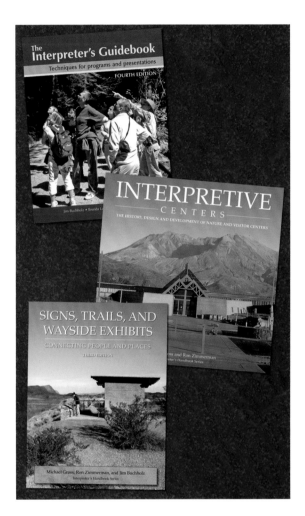

Ordering Books and Website Resources
www.interphandbooks.org

Visit the Interpreter's Handbook Series website at **www.interphandbooks.org** for special online resources and to order books. All proceeds from book sales support Schmeeckle Reserve and the UW-Stevens Point environmental education and interpretation program.

Index